THE ENEMY WITHIN

Ezra Levant

THE ENEMY WITHIN

*Terror, Lies, and the Whitewashing
of Omar Khadr*

McCLELLAND & STEWART

LIBRARY AND ARCHIVES CANADA CATALOGUING IN PUBLICATION

Levant, Ezra, 1972-
The enemy within : terror, lies, and the whitewashing
of Omar Khadr / Ezra Levant.

ISBN 978-0-7710-4600-1

1. Khadr, Omar, 1986–. 2. Political prisoners–Cuba–Guantánamo Bay Naval
Base–Biography. 3. Political prisoners–Legal status, laws, etc.– United States.
4. Canadians–Legal status, laws, etc.–United States. 5. Canada–Politics and
government–2006-. 6. War on Terrorism, 2001-2009. I. Title.

HV9468.K53L48 2011   341.6'50973   C2011-906029-9

We acknowledge the financial support of the Government of Canada through
the Book Publishing Industry Development Program and that of the Government
of Ontario through the Ontario Media Development Corporation's Ontario Book
Initiative. We further acknowledge the support of the Canada Council for the
Arts and the Ontario Arts Council for our publishing program.

All details contained in this book are current at the time of printing,
September 2011.

Published simultaneously in the United States of America by
McClelland & Stewart Ltd., P.O. Box 1030, Plattsburgh, New York 12901

Library of Congress Control Number: 2011936582

Typeset in Electra by M&S, Toronto
Printed and bound in Canada

This book is printed on acid-free paper that is 100% recycled,
ancient-forest friendly (100% post-consumer waste).

McClelland & Stewart Ltd.
75 Sherbourne Street
Toronto, Ontario
M5A 2P9
www.mcclelland.com

1   2   3   4   5   15   14   13   12   11

To the memory of Sgt. Christopher Speer

CONTENTS

CHAPTER 1

WHO IS OMAR KHADR?

"Omar Khadr stated in an interview with U.S. officials that a Jihad is occurring in Afghanistan and if non-believers enter a Muslim country then every Muslim in the world should fight the non-believers."

Confession of Omar Ahmed Khadr, October 13, 2010

1

Millions of Canadians know who Omar Khadr is. He's that handsome schoolboy with the peach fuzz and the black polo shirt we've seen innocently looking back at us from our morning paper for nearly a decade now. He seems so harmless. So young. So Canadian.

And that is what the morning papers, and the nightly news, and the left-wing websites, and Khadr's lawyers, political opportunists, and his family wanted you to see.

That famous photo, which appears to have come from his school yearbook, has been at the forefront of the Omar Khadr propaganda effort. It features large on the front cover of *Guantanamo's Child: The Untold Story of Omar Khadr*, a book whose very title frames the moist biography by Khadr's most ardent spin doctor, Michelle Shephard, a *Toronto Star* correspondent, who admits in the opening pages that far from being objective about the case – even though she was the *Star's* reporter covering the Khadr case since 2003 – she considers Khadr a "victim" of the injustice of the U.S. government that arrested and tried him for murdering an army medic, a victim of "retribution."[1] She also describes him as "an awkward puppy whose body hasn't yet caught up with its paws."[2] How adorable. How pitiful.

That wholesome-looking photo has become iconic. But there are other photos of Omar Khadr out there that you probably haven't seen, more recent ones than that shot taken when he was just twelve or thirteen years old. Other photos that weren't given to the press by his mother.[3] Seriously: that photograph, showing Khadr years younger than he really was when he joined al Qaeda, began building bombs, and then killed U.S. army medic Christopher Speer, was given to journalists like Shephard, and every other news outlet in the country, by Maha Khadr, his vile, hateful, terrorist-supporting mother. And they all accepted it and they all reprinted it, over and over again, deliberately passing over the far more recent – and far less innocent-looking – photographs.

There's the photo of Khadr posing next to an AK-47 assault rifle, dressed in the traditional *kameez* tunic and *kufi* hat preferred by Afghanistan's al Qaeda fighters. There's another one in which Omar is building bombs – improvised explosive devices (IEDs) – the same bombs that have killed nearly one hundred Canadian soldiers and *Calgary Herald* reporter Michelle Lang.

Those photos somehow never make it into the press coverage. Strangely, no matter what shocking and terrible facts have emerged over the years about Omar Khadr's commitment to terrorism, his deep dedication to killing Christians and Jews, and his passion for murder, editors across Canada have made the decision, time and time again, to run the photo of him in which he looks like an average Toronto pre-teen, the one handed to them directly from his mom. Some journalism.

From almost the moment Khadr was captured, Canada's liberal journalists have worked overtime to spin his story into something entirely detached from reality. No doubt it began as part of a media campaign to discredit the U.S. president at the time, George W. Bush, and the allied War on Terror, a journalistic instinct so visceral and overpowering that it resulted in the editor of the United Kingdom's *Daily Mirror* – Piers Morgan – being fired after printing fake photographs of allied soldiers supposedly abusing Muslim inmates. To the end, Morgan (now a primetime talk-show host on CNN, proving that crimes of leftist bias do pay in journalism) defended his fraud, insisting that the photos were sufficiently valid since he was sure soldiers were abusing Muslims somewhere.[4] That same journalistic crusade to undermine the War on Terror using false claims of "abuse" had *Newsweek* publish a fictional report about interrogators at Guantanamo Bay (Gitmo), the U.S. military's Cuban detention camp where Omar Khadr was detained, flushing a Koran down the toilet, supposedly to cause anguish to inmates. Fifteen people were killed, and dozens more injured, by the riots that false story set off in the Muslim world.[5]

The hatred that journalists have for America's – and Canada's – War on Terror, coupled with their insecure need to seem progressive and morally nuanced and, thus, sympathetic to Islamist terrorists, especially Omar Khadr, is what coloured their coverage of his imprisonment and trial as well. Every allegation of torture or abuse, no matter how baseless, was reported as if it had grounds; every threadbare claim by his family and lawyers about his innocence was given maximum play, while every solid piece of evidence proving the depths of Khadr's depravity and the convictions of his terrorism was buried – that's if it got reported at all. As you'll see in this book, there are scores of details about what Omar Khadr was really all about that never made it into the media.

This book will reveal the *actual* untold story of Omar Khadr – untold because it was so wantonly ignored by journalists across Canada. It will show you, with proof – not accusations, allegations, sob stories, or fabrications – that Khadr is anything but the immature, exploited little wayward lamb that his cheerleaders and propagandists have tried to portray him as. And it will show you why those corrupted portrayals have been every bit as dangerous as *Newsweek*'s fake Koran story, ensuring that Khadr was given a sweetheart deal so he could return to Canada even more radicalized than he was when he made the very conscious and deliberate decision to commit himself to jihad, to fight a holy war on the infidels. Khadr's own defence lawyers acknowledge that their client has yet to be deradicalized; he will return to Canada, after serving just a year of his sentence in Gitmo, as devoted to his bastardized, bloodthirsty interpretation of Islam as ever.

And even Omar Khadr himself admits things that the media won't. Forget the farrago of nonsense his lawyers have spread, with the media's eager complicity, about abuse at Guantanamo: Khadr has admitted that he's been treated gently by his American guards and interrogators, and evidence shows that far from being abused, he was actually coddled there. He confessed that he trained as an elite terrorist, and his study of poisons and political assassinations were clearly part of his plan to become a high-ranking international terrorist. He acknowledged that he supported and joined the worldwide terror campaign of al Qaeda, and that he did so on his own, not because his father wanted him to. Khadr admitted to leaping at the chance to kill Americans when it was offered to him, even when he could have just as easily opted out, and boasted that the proudest moments of his life were when he was building explosives to murder NATO soldiers. And he admitted that he was glad he got to kill an American and that, whenever he feels a bit gloomy, he cheers himself up by reminiscing about the joy he feels about that murder.

That is the deranged mind of Omar Khadr, every bit as demented as Paul Bernardo, Canada's infamous schoolgirl serial killer. When journalists covered the capture and detention of Bernardo, though, they were horrified. They had no sympathy for someone who could so casually and gleefully snuff out the life of another living, breathing human being for his own sick pleasure. But then, there was no grand political drama playing out as there is in the case of Omar Khadr. At least Khadr, finally, confessed to the depravity of his crimes, disappointing his fan club back home who had done all they could to have him exonerated;

Canadian journalists will never admit to the crime of deceit they committed in so irresponsibly torquing the real story about Khadr into something so fictitious.

In the end, all those news stories weren't really about Omar Khadr – not in the same way that the Bernardo coverage was actually about Paul Bernardo and his victims. That's why the victims in this case – U.S. Sgt. 1st Class Christopher Speer, his widowed wife, and two fatherless kids and the permanently wounded U.S. Sgt. 1st Class Layne Morris and his devastated family – have been virtually absent from the media's coverage of the Khadr case. This wasn't about terror or murder. Not to them. In the end, this was about denormalizing the War on Terror, Guantanamo Bay, the American military, the Canadian Security Intelligence Service, and, above all, U.S. president George W. Bush and, later, Canadian prime minister Stephen Harper.

In the newsrooms of the nation, the Omar Khadr story was actually about turning our defenders into war criminals and Khadr and his al Qaeda comrades, who commit real war crimes, into victims. Khadr is an enemy of Canada because he has dedicated himself to prosecuting al Qaeda's war of terror against Western countries, including ours; but his gang of Canadian supporters, propagandists, and apologists are also guilty of undermining Canadians' security. They, too, have proven themselves enemies in our midst. This is what Richard Fadden, the head of the Canadian Security Intelligence Service (CSIS), meant when he lamented that "those accused of terrorist offenses [are] often portrayed in the media as quasi folk heroes" and that a "loose partnership of single-issues NGOs, advocacy journalists and lawyers" had succeeded "in forging a positive public image for anyone accused of terrorist links or charges."[6] Fadden understands the importance of national security. He also understands how it can be insidiously subverted from within.

Before long, Khadr will be back in Canada, and may well be released, thanks to a lenient system that will likely credit him for the time he's served awaiting trial in Gitmo. And when Omar Khadr is back on Canadian streets, as radical, unrepentant, and dangerous as he's ever been, the journalists and activists who worked so hard to get him freed can give themselves a well-earned pat on the back.

It will be the rest of us who will be left to deal with it.

CHAPTER 2

TERRORISM: THE KHADR FAMILY BUSINESS

"Omar Khadr indicated that following September 11, 2001, he was told about a $1,500 reward placed on each American killed. Omar Khadr indicated that when he heard about the reward, he wanted to kill a lot of American[s] to get lots of money."

Confession of Omar Ahmed Khadr, October 13, 2010

When America first met Omar Khadr, on July 27, 2002, he had a simple message for the Special Forces soldiers who found him, heavily wounded and bleeding, among the rubble of a bombed-out al Qaeda compound in Khost, Afghanistan.

"Fuck you, Americans," he said. "Shoot me."[1]

The troops had, in fact, already shot Khadr twice. They had come upon him in an al Qaeda–run compound in Khost, southeast of Kabul, after a bloody four-hour firefight with Khadr and his al Qaeda comrades. U.S. forces had spent an entire morning raking the compound with bullets while F-18s clobbered it with massive five-hundred-pound bombs. They had repeatedly urged those inside to get out, and many people took advantage of that offer, including the women and children, and were provided cover by American soldiers as they fled. When the return fire stopped and U.S. troops approached the compound to look in on the dead and wounded, Khadr ambushed them, lobbing a grenade, mortally wounding U.S. Sgt. 1st Class Christopher Speer. Lucky for Khadr, when U.S. soldiers fired back on the fifteen-year-old Canadian to disable him, they stopped short of killing him.

But Omar Khadr wanted to die anyway.

"Fuck you, Americans," he said. "Shoot me."

He wanted to die a martyr.

This is the kind of death that Islamist terrorists dream of – going out in a blaze of glory after murdering as many Christians or Jews as they are able to. "That wasn't a panicky teenager we encountered that day," said U.S. Sgt. 1st Class Layne Morris, who lost his right eye in the four-hour battle with Khadr and his comrades. "That was a trained al Qaeda agent who wanted to make his last act on Earth the killing of an American."[2]

Omar Khadr had spent much time with his father discussing their wish to die fighting a jihad and the wonderful rewards that Allah would provide them in the afterlife.[3] There would probably be the standard seventy-two virgins. Omar would be very interested in those, of course. But they had fun imagining what other rewards awaited them for their earthly work of slaughtering infidels. Beautiful waterfalls. Elephants. A swimming pool filled with Jell-O, Omar's favourite dessert. Terrorism was the Khadr family business, and Omar was enthusiastic about reaping its rewards.

No one in the Khadr family was pushed into making themselves into enemies of Canada. They did it by choice. In fact, Ahmed Said and Maha Khadr, Omar's parents, had the kinds of opportunities that millions of people all over the world can only hope for. Ahmed was born in Egypt, but the Canadian government allowed him to immigrate to Ontario in 1977; Maha was born a Palestinian but was given the same gift: the privilege to move to one of the healthiest, wealthiest, freest countries on Earth. Her parents opened a bakery in Toronto that became very popular and they made something of themselves. Maha's opportunities were bright.

Ahmed got to attend the University of Ottawa, where he studied computer engineering, the cost of his education offset by the generous subsidies of Canadian taxpayers. He landed a job consulting for Bell Northern Research, a top-notch telecommunications firm owned jointly by Bell Canada and Northern Telecom, the company that would eventually become known as Nortel and one of the most dynamic and successful stock market darlings of the dot-com era. In the late 1970s, Ahmed was well placed for the dawn of the high-tech age, thanks to the enviable opportunities offered in his new Canadian home. A year before Ahmed arrived in North America, a man named Bill Gates had incorporated a firm he called Microsoft, and another man named Steve Jobs incorporated a company called Apple Inc. For computer engineers, the opportunities were about to become limitless.

But Ahmed Khadr wasn't interested in following the path of his in-laws: building a good career, providing for his family, and being a responsible Canadian. The family hardly spent time in Canada, moving instead between Pakistan and Afghanistan. Occassionally they'd send the kids to stay with their grandparents in Toronto, or return to Canada for a vacation, or when Ahmed had some business to take care of, or when they needed access to sophisticated and free health care (one of the Khadr sons had a serious heart defect and the family readily availed themselves of the top-flight surgeons at Toronto's Hospital for Sick Children), or when things got dicey and they needed a safe haven. Mother Maha Khadr was revolted by Canada and despised the thought of raising a son here, where "by the time he's 12 or 13 he'll be on drugs or having some homosexual relation or this and that."[4] The Khadrs hated Canada. They wanted their citizenship for just one thing: as a convenient tool they could exploit to promote criminal Islamic jihad.

By any definition, the Khadrs are a crime family – the Scarfaces of Scarborough, the Jihad Mafia. "I admit it that we are an al Qaeda family," Omar's older brother told the Canadian Broadcasting Corporation (CBC) in 2005. No, they didn't bootleg liquor, smuggle drugs, run gambling dens, or traffic prostitutes like Tony Soprano or Vito Corleone. Such things were beneath Godfather Ahmed Khadr, who considered himself too pious, too good a Muslim to dirty his hands with anything *haraam* (forbidden by the Muslim faith), like liquor or casinos. The Khadr family had a different racket: defrauding Canadian donors using a charity front group and then funnelling the money to jihadists overseas so they could build bombs and buy guns to murder infidels. In the Khadrs' version of piety, there was nothing wrong with that at all.

Whenever the Khadrs would find themselves reluctantly having to visit Canada, Ahmed would hit the mosque circuit, raising money for charities. At first, it all seemed legitimate enough. For a few years in the early

1980s, Ahmed at least looked like he was raising funds to support the families of Afghanistan that had been devastated by the Soviet invasion. Money raised in Canada, he'd claim, would buy shares of sheep or cows so that families left fatherless might eat; it might buy artificial limbs for children disfigured by landmines.

By 1986, however, it was clear that Ahmed wasn't simply helping the orphans of Afghanistan that had been maimed by Soviet landmines. Suddenly, he was hanging around with a man by the name of Ayman al-Zawahiri. If you recognize that name, it's for good reason: Zawahiri would go on to become the second-in-command to Osama bin Laden in the al Qaeda organization.

When he connected with Ahmed Khadr, Zawahiri was already highly radicalized, a senior member of the Egyptian Islamic Jihad, one of the militant Muslim groups working to overthrow the Western-friendly Egyptian government and replace it with an Islamic theocracy. One of Zawahiri's collaborators at the time, Omar Abdel-Rahman, or the Blind Sheik as he's popularly known, is one of the world's arch terrorists, behind the deaths of more than a thousand people, including the massacre of fifty-eight tourists in Luxor, Egypt, in 1997. Rahman is also credited with being the man who ordered the fatwa on Egyptian president Anwar Sadat, who dared to make peace with the Jews in Israel, inspiring a group of army officers to assassinate Sadat in 1981. After the assassination, both Rahman and Zawahiri were rounded up by government agents and put on trial. During the hearing, Zawahiri announced to the world's media, in fluent English, his crusade to turn Egypt into an Islamic state, while all around him his fellow prisoners shouted, "We will not sacrifice the blood of Muslims for the Americans and the Jews."[5] After serving three years, Zawahiri was released. Being a surgeon, he then travelled to Peshawar to operate on the wounded Mujahideen, the Islamist fighters rebelling against the Soviet occupation. It was there that he met Ahmed Khadr and discovered their mutual interest: their desire to see Islam become the one and only authority in the world.[6] It was a vision that they knew would demand copious violence.

By the late 1980s, with their "holy war" against the U.S.S.R. nearly finished, Islamists were readying for somewhere new to direct their jihad, to build on their success in Afghanistan, and to leverage the infrastructure they had built to battle the infidel Soviets. Ahmed Khadr had by then become a well-respected figure in Osama bin Laden's organization, a group that would soon begin to call itself al Qaeda.

For years, Ahmed had represented himself in Canada as a man of mercy: he toured the mosques of Toronto pleading for help for the pitiable children of Afghanistan, the poor souls who had been made collateral damage by the invasion of an aggressive imperialist force. On more than one occasion, he waxed forlorn to the *Toronto Star*, which covered his fundraising tours with earnest sympathy. As the war ended, the true character of Khadr's mission began to reveal itself. Anyone truly concerned about the suffering of children in a war-torn country would desire an end to war. But that's not quite what Ahmed wanted. Peace wasn't enough for the godfather of the Jihadi Mafia. He wanted there to be more conflict. He wanted more fighting, until he won the prize that he dreamed of: the supremacy of Islam. This was no longer about widows and orphans; it had become clear that Ahmed's racket wasn't really about the war in Afghanistan. "Afghanistan's cause is not an Afghan cause," he declared in a speech he gave to a crowd at the Markham Islamic Centre, north of Toronto. "It's your cause. It's my cause too. It's every Muslim's cause."[7] For Ahmed Khadr, the battle would not be won until Muslims had established a truly Islamic government, like the terrorist-supporting Taliban he was fighting for.

The Canadian government was suspicious about the stories suggesting that Human Concern International (HCI), the supposed aid organization started by a pair of Calgary Muslims that Ahmed Khadr worked for, was really all about supporting the wounded kids of Afghanistan. The Canadian Security and Intelligence Service (CSIS) had prepared a report on HCI for the federal government's foreign aid arm. Stewart Bell, a reporter at Canada's *National Post* newspaper, saw a copy of it, though, he reported, it was too heavily censored to reveal any information specifically about Ahmed Khadr. But it did detail how alleged Islamic aid organizations like HCI had been misrepresenting their work and were actually used as a critical "means of channeling ostensibly humanitarian relief funds to the Arab Mujahedin [rebels] in Afghanistan and Pakistan."[8] The United States Central Intelligence Agency (CIA), meanwhile, had come to much the same conclusion about HCI's dodgy nature. In a 1996 report, the CIA disclosed that the entire branch of HCI that was run by Khadr in Peshawar, Pakistan, was a nerve centre of Islamist militants, while HCI's Swedish branch was involved in smuggling weapons to Bosnia. In an interview with an Egyptian journalist, it was none other than Osama bin Laden who identified Human Concern International as a significant supporter of al Qaeda.[9]

So, Canadians who had read in the *Toronto Star* the tearful pleas of Ahmed Khadr and others like him, asking for help for the most vulnerable people caught in the cross-fire of a brutal war, and sent money to groups like HCI were being used. Unwittingly, good-natured Canadians appear to have ended up buying guns, and ammunition, and bombs, and anti-aircraft weapons, and landmines for jihad-ist guerrillas. The Canadian government, which awarded international aid grants to HCI for a time, was presumably hoodwinked too. Men like Ahmed Khadr, who claimed to be interested only in helping the innocent victims of war and terror, were actually perpetuating it.

According to Khadr family lore, in 1992, with the Soviets gone, Ahmed was fighting in a civil war to control who would get to run Afghanistan – the communist government of Mohammad Najibullah, the warlords, or the Islamists – when he was hit by a bomb and seriously wounded. Naturally, the doctors in Pakistan weren't good enough for an elite family of terrorists like the Khadrs.

They flew back to Toronto so that Ahmed could have his arm saved by top Canadian surgeons. Friends urged him to stay in Toronto; the Soviets were gone, after all, and he had, so they believed, done more than enough for the people of Afghanistan. After his brush with death, he should take it easy and enjoy a more comfortable life in Ontario. But he didn't want to stay. He didn't like it. A biography praising Khadr on an al Qaeda website said the patriarch didn't like the "dirty swamp" that was Canada.[10] Instead, he raced back to Pakistan. Once there, he sent his sons off to training camps in Afghanistan. A spy for the British and French intelligence services had infiltrated the training camp, and the spy remembers the Khadr father coming to visit the camp on one occasion.[11] He didn't come to visit his sons, though: he was seen disappearing into the explosives laboratory. What he was up to would become vividly and violently clear very soon.

That was in 1994, when Ayman al-Zawahiri was planning to begin his next phase of terror, having now allied himself with Osama bin Laden. At 9:30 a.m. on November 19, 1995, the plan went into action.[12] Two men approached the Egyptian Embassy in Islamabad, Pakistan. One attacked the guards with machine-gun fire and grenades, murdering them. The other careened a pickup truck loaded up with 250 pounds of explosives toward the gates and detonated the bomb, blowing open the barriers. Then came a jeep, with even more explosives. It pulled up alongside the building and exploded, destroying the side of the embassy. Fourteen people were murdered that day, and sixty were wounded. The two bombers also died.

Investigators were able to use the engine block of one of the vehicles employed in the terrorist attack to trace the perpetrators. One of the men the trail led to was Khalid Abdullah. Abdullah was the fiancé of Zaynab Khadr, Ahmed's eldest daughter. The Khadr patriarch had arranged the marriage when Zaynab was just fifteen years old.[13] Abdullah had been behind the purchase of one of the vehicles used in the terrorist operation. He had been living with Ahmed and was a part of the Khadr crime family business. But police couldn't arrest him: Abdullah had skipped town after the embassy bombing. They did try arresting his accomplice, Ahmed Khadr. When they showed up, Maha tried to block the door and Zaynab pulled a gun on them. Authorities would find $40,000 in cold, hard U.S. cash in the Khadr house.[14] The Khadrs claimed it was for charity.

The Khadrs were prepared to face down Pakistani security forces at gunpoint, dying as martyrs for their Islamic cause. They just weren't prepared to serve jail time. Ahmed was once quoted in an article in *Rolling Stone* magazine telling his family "if you love me, pray that I will get martyred."[15] He didn't say anything about what they should do if he was arrested on terrorism charges. But they had an idea.

Once again, they would exploit their Canadian citizenship as a tool to preserve their terrorist enterprise. After he was taken into Pakistani custody, Ahmed Khadr declared he would go on a hunger strike. "I'm Canadian. I am

100 per cent innocent person," he told reporters who visited him while he was under guard at an Islamabad hospital.[16]

By sheer luck, in early 1996, while Pakistani authorities were holding and interrogating Ahmed Khadr about his role in the embassy bombing, the prime minister of Canada happened to be visiting Islamabad. Jean Chrétien had come to Pakistan on a Team Canada trade mission, along with provincial premiers, professors, top Canadian business leaders, and, of course, a pack of journalists hungry for good stories. The Khadrs knew exactly how to play this opportunity. Even before Chrétien had left Canadian soil, Ahmed Khadr was spinning a sob story for the Canadian press. The always credulous *Toronto Star* ran a sympathetic story on Khadr's detention and his hunger strike. He wanted, more than anything, to go back to Canada, he pleaded, not mentioning how little interest he'd had in living there before. "The last hope I have is Mr. Chrétien coming," he said.

Then he cannily pointed out that Canada was a major aid donor to Pakistan – one of the biggest, actually. "We have leverage," he said.[17] Did they ever.

And so Mother Khadr dragged her doe-eyed children to the hotel where Chrétien was staying to plead with him, to confront him in the presence of all those watchful journalists. The prime minister should have been suspicious. He certainly had legitimate grounds to tell her politely there was nothing he could do. By then, the Canadian government was already wise to the corrupt dealings of Ahmed Khadr. As early as the late 1980s, federal officials were informed by Chinese diplomats that their fellow Canadian had been smuggling cash from Saudi Arabia, home of Osama bin Laden's family fortune, into Afghanistan, and Khadr had gotten tripped up in a border incident while passing through the Pakistani province of Balochistan. This was "not the first time that Khadr had been involved in money running," the Chinese informed Canadian officials. The prime minister's handlers knew that Canadian authorities had also got reports from Pakistan's intelligence services revealing the burgeoning partnership between Khadr and the notorious terrorist and head of Egyptian Islamic Jihad, Ayman al-Zawahiri.[18]

And there was all that intel on Khadr's supposed charity work. After the Soviets had been driven out of Afghanistan, Ottawa wasn't certain it could prove that Human Concern International was funnelling money to extremist Muslims still fighting to establish a theocratic Islamic state that would provide safe haven to terrorists like Osama bin Laden and Ayman al-Zawahiri – something that would eventually come to pass once the Taliban had prevailed – but its suspicions were serious enough that it cut all funding to HCI. The "aid" organization tried suing the government to get its federal subsidies restored. The Canadian government fought fiercely through the courts to distance itself from HCI.[19] And the government won.

But Jean Chrétien was a softer touch. Already, the prime minister was being widely criticized and was under pressure from Canadian conservatives for his stubborn refusal when travelling to countries like China and Arab nations to bring up human rights abuses. When Maha Khadr came barging in with all those little kids sobbing about the plight of her poor, victimized husband at the hands of Pakistan's cruel interrogators – they had pulled his hair and beard, Khadr had claimed – Chrétien invited her to share her concerns. He fed the children candy. He posed for photographs with them. He told them, "Once, I was the son of a farmer and I became prime minister. Maybe one day you will become one."[20]

Back home, the newspapers, naive and ignorant of what federal intelligence officials – and even Chrétien's own staff – knew about the Khadr family's links to terror, painted a sympathetic picture of a man made victim of a terrible injustice. As James Bartleman, one of the prime minister's political advisors who would later become the lieutenant governor of Ontario, recalled in his memoir, journalists travelling with the Team Canada mission were "tired" of reporting on the daily grip-and-grin meetings between business and political leaders. "All hungered for a good juicy scandal to enliven their reporting." The Khadrs had given it to them, he wrote, "complete with photogenic wife, cute children, and brave Canadian husband suffering in a prison hospital."[21]

Despite all the red flags the Canadian government had thrown up over the Khadrs, Chrétien went ahead and personally took up the cause of the al Qaeda family: during a meeting with the prime minister of Pakistan, Benazir Bhutto, Chrétien took the time to raise his concerns about Ahmed Khadr. He wanted assurances that the Pakistani government was behaving fairly, that they were treating him according to the standards Canada expected prisoners should be treated. "I wanted to make very clear that due process is followed in this case," Chrétien told reporters.[22]

Of course, the high standards that Canada adheres to for due process are uncommon in the world, and particularly unusual in a place like Pakistan, where the worst criminals aren't murderers but incorrigible mass murderers: terrorists who will shoot up a mosque without feeling a pang of guilt, who will blow up a school, with pride, and be glorified for it. They work in secretive terrorist cells; they are trained to resist interrogation, trained to complain of fictional torture. It's easy to criticize the abuses of the Pakistani justice system, and there are surely abuses. But it's not so easy to imagine a system like Canada's effectively dealing with the kind, and sheer number, of terrorists that Pakistan's must deal with. The South Asia Intelligence Group has identified no fewer than forty-seven different terrorist groups operating in Pakistan.[23] In 2008, the U.S. State Department counted 1,839 terrorist incidents in Pakistan.[24]

For police to detain a suspect in Canada without sufficient evidence of their crime is intolerable: we know that the risks to our society of that kind of practice outweigh the risks that a car thief or a marijuana dealer or even a murderer might pose if he or she were let go. The way they see things in Pakistan, when police release a suspected terrorist because they haven't yet built an airtight case against him, it could very well mean hundreds of people will be dead or wounded by the end of the week. This is, after all, exactly what the entire debate around Guantanamo Bay and Omar Khadr is about: how the law should deal with avowed enemies who play by different rules than normal criminals.

But this was 1996. In the pre–9/11 era, Jean Chrétien, like many North Americans, perhaps was blissfully unfamiliar with the duplicity and menace posed by jihadis like Ahmed Khadr and with the special challenge they posed to prosecutors. And so, Chrétien pressed Pakistani prime minister Bhutto, wanting to be sure they had proof positive that Ahmed Khadr was one of the terrorists behind the Egyptian Embassy bombing. Bhutto, like the Khadr family, knew her country relied heavily on Canadian aid. She knew Canadians had "leverage," as Ahmed Khadr put it. Shortly after she met Chrétien, Ahmed Khadr was released.

Khadr did not, however, retire to Canada, as he had claimed he so badly wanted to do. In fact, it wasn't long before he moved the whole family to Jalalabad, Afghanistan, to a compound run by none other than Osama bin Laden.[25]

The Pakistanis and the Egyptians never stopped believing Ahmed Khadr was one of the terrorist organizers behind that bloody attack in Islamabad.

"They were terrorists, confirmed terrorists," Major-Gen. Shaukat Sultan Khan, a spokesperson for the Pakistan army, revealed to the National Post years later. "Their involvement in terrorist activities was proved beyond doubt."[26]

In fact, when the United States invaded Afghanistan in 2001 and Khadr was forced to flee back into Pakistan, he would die in a gun battle with police, who had been sent, again, to arrest him. Pakistan knew all along that Ahmed Khadr was a man with blood all over his hands. Canadian intelligence officials had a pretty good idea too. If it hadn't been for the naïveté of the Canadian press and a PR-sensitive Canadian prime minister, he might have been stopped before he was able to bloody his hands even more. Instead, Ahmed Khadr's family became one of the most valuable crews inside Osama bin Laden's multi-national terrorist organization.

After Ahmed Khadr died in 2003, the Canadian public finally began learning the ugly truth about the Khadr crime family. They learned that all the charity work that the Khadrs had been supposedly running was a scam. In Afghanistan and Pakistan throughout the 1980s, a man named Mohamed Fadil worked for Khadr at the group that would later call itself Human Concern International.[27] After Khadr's death, Fadil went public about the fraud Khadr was running: the charity was registered as Canadian, but the main funding – as much as $3 million every single month – came from the Kuwaiti group Lajnat Al-Da'wa al Islamia, which was identified in a 2001 U.S. presidential Executive Order as supporting terrorists.[28]

Fadil finally exposed what really went on in the Khadrs' charity, which included paying salaries to Egyptian terrorists – among them a man named Abu Khabab, one of al Qaeda's top weapons experts, who was working on building chemical and biological bombs[29] – and providing advice to Osama bin Laden and al Qaeda's number-two man, Ayman al-Zawahiri. Fadil revealed that Khadr used his charity office, and the money raised for it, to provide a haven for dozens of Egyptian jihadis transiting to Afghanistan. One of the men who passed through Khadr's office was Khalid Sheik Mohamed, considered al Qaeda's chief architect behind the 9/11 attacks.

Intelligence by CSIS backs Fadil up: a report by the spy agency examined by a federal court judge in 2005 detailed how Khadr – the "head of a family of Islamic extremists" – "provided references" to al Qaeda for jihadis "wishing to partake in extremist training in Afghanistan" and "was the director of an aid agency known as Human Concern International, which worked closely with al Qaeda in Afghanistan."[30]

"Khadr was really a jihadi," Fadil told the *National Post* in 2010. "Khadr was not a charity worker." In fact, he says, even the Kuwaiti funders grew tired of Khadr's single-minded obsession with fighting jihad: they fired him in 1986 because he was neglecting the other duties they needed him to work on. It's little wonder that in its *Book of 120 Martyrs in Afghanistan*, the al-Fajr Media Centre, a pro-terrorist propaganda office, portrayed Ahmed Khadr as always bored in Canada because "his soul was accustomed to calamities and fighting infidels."[31] For Khadr, jihad was a "full-time" preoccupation, Fadil told the *National Post*, adding that Khadr was indeed part of the embassy bombing plot. Khadr's charity work was also linked to Benevolence International, a North American charity that also claimed to be raising money for widows and orphans but whose founder pleaded guilty in 2003 to funnelling money to al Qaeda–connected Islamic fighters in Bosnia and Chechnya.[32]

And Khadr didn't just provide money, advice, and safe houses to terrorists. It appears he actually ran a terrorist unit of his own. In 2006, Islamist websites began boasting of the successes of the Mahdi Army's rocket attacks against coalition forces. "Ahmed Said Khadr," they wrote, "used to be in charge of it."[33]

That is certainly consistent with what the Royal Canadian Mounted Police (RCMP) has revealed about Ahmed Khadr's last years on the run, in Afghanistan and Taliban-friendly Pakistan, from U.S.–backed forces. The RCMP has said that Khadr was ordered by Osama bin Laden to form a militia force and organize "attacks against U.S. and coalition forces" near the Pakistan–Afghanistan border.[34]

In fact, the RCMP didn't suspect that just Ahmed Khadr was a key part of Osama bin Laden's growing terror network, they observed the whole Khadr gang getting involved. "I believe that the entire family is affiliated with al-Qaeda and has participated in some form or another with these criminal extremist elements," RCMP Sgt. Konrad Shourie, one of Canada's top terror investigators, declared in an affidavit in 2005.[35]

Ahmed's oldest son, Abdullah Khadr, admitted to buying weapons for al Qaeda – $20,000 worth of explosives, rocket-propelled grenades, machine-gun ammunition, and mortars[36] – and even bought a black market passport so he could hide out in China or Iran (two countries that do not have extradition treaties with the United States) after the fall of Afghanistan, though he was reportedly "too afraid to use it."[37] The FBI got Abdullah to admit he channelled hydrogen peroxide (used to make landmines), C-4 explosives, surface-to-air missiles, anti-tank missiles, and AK-47s to al Qaeda.[38] RCMP and FBI officers have also produced Abdullah's confession that he was working on a plot to kill Pakistan's pro-Western prime minister. Abdullah had reportedly told a journalist in Pakistan he wanted to die a "martyr" for his religion,[39] but the Khadr crime family wasn't just in it for Allah – they were out to make a profit in the bloody business of terror too. When Abdullah was arrested in Pakistan in 2004, he was buying missiles from an ex-member of a Pakistani terror group for $1,000 each. He was planning to resell them to an al Qaeda buyer for $5,000 a pop.[40] Like his dad, Ahmed Khadr, Abdullah turned terror into a money-making enterprise.

Then there's the oldest Khadr daughter, Zaynab. She, along with Abdullah and her mother, Maha, acted as a courier by delivering money to her father to "fund and supply al-Qaeda camps in Afghanistan," according to the RCMP.[41] (After her brother Omar's capture by U.S. forces, she dismissed his murder of Sgt. 1st Class Christopher Speer as "no big deal."[42]) Zaynab "willingly participated and contributed both directly and indirectly toward enhancing the ability of al-Qaeda to facilitate its criminal activities," the police force determined. Meanwhile, another son, Kareem Khadr, who was partly paralyzed in the gun battle with Pakistani security forces that killed his father in 2003, appears to be into criminal activity that's a whole different kind of seedy: in 2010, he was arrested in Toronto for the alleged sexual exploitation of a minor.[43]

And then there's Omar, the favoured son of the Khadr crime family,[44] the Michael to Ahmed's Don Corleone. By 2004, nearly two years after having rescued him from that demolished al Qaeda compound, the U.S. military had already got details out of Omar about his own role in the Canadian-run branch plant of al Qaeda's terrorist enterprise. Omar had admitted that he was trained as an al Qaeda terrorist, acted as a translator for al Qaeda – because he spoke English and Pashto, the main language in Afghanistan – and was actively working to "blow up" American soldiers.[45] He conducted surveillance missions for al Qaeda planners to prepare attacks on NATO military convoys.

Omar was climbing the ladder in his father's dirty business. He knew all about what his dear old dad was up to: he "provided U.S. officials with significant details regarding the operation of the training camps, including the fact that his father was responsible for providing financing for these camps, other al Qaeda sponsored camps, and other sponsored activities," as he states in his very own confession.[46]

And the young man was certainly preparing to become one of the best in his field. He took individual tutoring to become a terrorist from an al Qaeda guru who gave him "training in the use of rocket propelled grenades, various assault rifles, pistols, grenades, and explosives." He joined an al Qaeda terrorist cell, where he worked to convert Italian landmines into improvised explosive devices (IEDs). He called building these bombs "the proudest moment of his life" because they would "cause as much death and destruction as possible." He was told there was a $1,500 reward for every American he killed. He told his captors that when he heard that, "he wanted to kill a lot of American[s], to get lots of money."[47]

Ahmed Khadr, Zaynab Khadr, Omar Khadr, and others of the Khadr clan talked a lot about martyrdom and wanting to die for Islam while fighting a jihad against the Jews and the infidels. Every crime family has its Old World codes of honour; in the mafia they take "blood oaths"; in this gang, it's martyrdom oaths. And that, ultimately, is what the Khadr family proved itself to be: a criminal dynasty making a living through the family business of money laundering, fraud, arms trafficking, and, of course, murder. It wasn't something any of them needed to do: one of Omar's brothers, Abdurahman Khadr, wasn't as interested as the rest of his siblings and ended up turning his back on the enterprise. He preferred Toronto to the dusty mud compounds of Peshawar and Kabul, was uninterested in the terrorist training camps his father kept sending him off to, wasn't impressed by Osama bin Laden, and didn't buy into the rotten business promoted by the rest of his family.[48] He didn't aspire to become a productive member of Khadr Murder Inc.

Not like his brother Omar.

CHAPTER 3

THE ECSTATIC MURDERER

"Khadr and the other operatives in the cell targeted U.S. forces with the specific intent of killing Americans, and as many as possible. Over the course of multiple interviews with U.S. personnel, Omar Khadr described in great detail the making and planting of the IEDs and the destruction that he and the other cell members hoped would be caused by the explosions. When asked why he and the other cell members were constructing IEDs, Khadr stated 'to kill U.S. forces.' Omar Khadr stated to a U.S. official that the proudest moment of his life was constructing and planting IEDs."

Confession of Omar Ahmed Khadr, October 13, 2010

W hat's the proudest moment of your life?

Ask most Canadians that question and you're bound to hear about a lot of great things people have done. Maybe getting a diploma or a degree of some sort, or seeing a son or daughter get one. Finishing a marathon, perhaps. Getting that dream job. Taking the oath of citizenship. Helping someone in trouble get his or her life back on the right track. Beating cancer. Walking your daughter down the aisle at her wedding. Even from teenagers, you'd probably hear about the day they made the basketball team or the cheerleading squad, or performed the lead in the school play, or when they brought home a really great report card, or got into the college they really wanted to attend.

And if you asked Omar Khadr what the proudest moment in his life was? Well, that we already know. We know from his eventual confession of his crimes, the agreed facts he signed as part of his plea deal with U.S. military prosecutors in 2010, that he told U.S. officials all about it.[1] Khadr said that "the proudest moment of his life was constructing and planting IEDs," or improvised explosive devices, which he and his fellow terrorists planted in the ground "to kill U.S. forces." He was proud, he said, of the opportunity to kill "as many as possible" to "maximize the opportunity for death and destruction."

Meet the real Omar Khadr. No, this isn't the poor, wayward little lamb dragooned by his father into the al Qaeda racket as portrayed by his sympathizers in the media. This is Omar Khadr, the bloodthirsty warrior, the enthusiastic criminal, the eager terrorist, the ecstatic murderer.

By the time Omar Khadr finally came clean about his crimes, the Canadian media had already worked up their own, preferred version of who they thought he was – or at least who they wanted him to be. Nothing – not even the eventual black-and-white proof of Khadr's viciousness – would change their minds. Khadr would inevitably fess up about his lust for blood and chaos, though, in his detailed confession to the court at Guantanamo, signing his name to a document that provided the true, full picture of how depraved his thinking was and what his actual, sadistic ambitions really were.

Omar Khadr, after all, was different than most of the young men who turned up at al Qaeda training camps to join the army of jihad. The average Pakistani or Yemeni villager doesn't have the blessings that come with a Canadian passport, for one thing, and so they can hardly dare to imagine the kind of fortunate life packed with opportunities that is there for the taking for a Canadian citizen like Omar Khadr. There aren't a lot of good jobs in Amran or Waziristan, no top-tier universities offering heavily subsidized spots to anyone ready to put in a little effort like they do in Canada. For a lot of al Qaeda fighters, the choice to join jihad may at least have been partly understandable in that it might look to them like the best of an awfully lousy lot of choices.

It's also possible to understand why, if you've never actually met a Westerner in your life, or seen a Jewish person, or been exposed to the reality of Christianity, you might believe the monstrous tales your village imam tells you. There aren't actual Jewish people living in Afghanistan or Pakistan. With nothing more than a third-grade education, the average poppy farmer probably is open to believing that Jews murder babies for their matzo and conspire to manipulate the world for its gold; it's a lot easier to convince someone who doesn't know much about the contemporary world or its history that Christians really are savage crusaders out to conquer Muslim lands and convert Mohammedans to Christianity by force. In 2010, the Pew Research Center's Global Attitudes Surveyed measured how Muslims in the Middle East perceived Jews.[2] Not surprisingly, in the lands where Jewish people haven't lived for generations – exiled as they were by Muslim governments – negative feeling toward Jews was the highest. In Judenrein ("Jewish-free") Jordan, 97 per cent of people thought badly of Jews, in Judenrein Egypt, it was 95 per cent. The only Middle Eastern Muslims who thought positively of Jews, of course, were Israeli Arabs, where a majority of people surveyed had positive views about Jews. That's because Israeli Arabs actually live among Jews and so don't imagine them as rat-faced monsters with blood

34

dripping from their fangs, which is the way they're typically portrayed in the Arab press.

These are the huge advantages Omar Khadr had over his fellow jihadis. He'd grown up in Toronto. He knew the truth about Westerners. He was raised in a city with the eleventh-biggest population of Jewish people in the world outside of Israel.[3] He saw hundreds of Jewish and Christian and Hindu and Buddhist people every day and witnessed their normalcy and, no doubt, their natural friendliness, peacefulness, and kindness. And he knew that in Canada, different religions and races get along just fine. The Toronto bakery owned by his grandparents was next to a Jamaican restaurant and an optical shop owned by a pair of brothers from Guyana;[4] Eglinton Avenue, where the bakery sat, must easily be one of the most ethnically diverse strips of commerce in North America. And those grandparents, Mohamed and Fatmah Elsamnah, with whom Omar spent parts of his childhood as his father was busy building terror networks abroad, were, it certainly seems, happy immigrants, contented with their adopted home of Canada and very much against the idea of their daughter and her kids relocating to Pakistan when Canada had so much peace, security, and prosperity to offer.[5]

Omar Khadr, in other words, wasn't ignorant. He wasn't the victim of propaganda. He knew the truth about how the world worked, the kind of people that non–Muslim Westerners really are, and the peaceful, just world that they seek. And he dedicated his life to killing them anyway.

In fact, based on what he finally confessed about his plans and his crimes, it certainly seems that Omar Khadr was preparing to become a top dog of terror. His father was reportedly already the fourth-in-command in the al Qaeda organization;[6] Omar can only have imagined himself rising to even greater, more murderous criminal heights.

Omar admitted that already as he was growing up, he spent a great deal of time meeting "senior al Qaeda leaders, including Usama bin Laden, Dr. [Ayman al-] Zawahiri, Muhammed Atef [al Qaeda's military chief], and Saif al Adel," the explosives expert rumoured to be bin Laden's successor as the leader of al Qaeda, following bin Laden's death.[7] Omar "visited various al Qaeda training camps, guest houses, and safe houses," where he must have been impressed by these characters, finding them the perfect role models for an aspiring young terrorist. While an average Canadian boy might have looked at these murderous men, squatted in their mud huts, spewing hatred and misogyny and plotting the death of innocents on a grand scale, and easily preferred the options on offer in Canada – the good schools, the career opportunities, the healthy and serene lifestyle, the love of peace – Omar Khadr, it seems, was enamoured with joining their criminal death cult. Smart, educated, worldly, and with all the right family connections, he had to have envisioned himself rising to the very top of the world's most racist, most brutal criminal organization.

And he couldn't wait.

It's certainly clear from his confession that Omar Khadr wasn't planning to become just another low-level foot soldier in the al Qaeda organization. Not with the kind of training he was getting. In his confession, Khadr details the al Qaeda training camps that he visited and the tactics being taught there. This wasn't only about how to handle an AK-47 or detonate a landmine on some Afghan dirt road. This was much, much bigger stuff.

When he was at the Derunta camp, for instance, men were trained in "explosives and poisons." At the Khaldan camp where Khadr spent time, he explained how they trained al Qaeda recruits in "poisons, sabotage, target selection, urban warfare and assassination tactics." Now, it's probably safe to say that poisons wouldn't be of much use in the Afghan theatre of war: there just aren't that many opportunities for a Taliban soldier to spike a crusading U.S. soldier's water bottle with strychnine or sprinkle rat poison on his or her meal rations. But U.S. intelligence officials did reveal in late 2010 that al Qaeda operatives have been working on a potential attack in North America that would kill innocent civilians by contaminating public salad bars and buffets at hotels and restaurants with ricin or cyanide.[8] The intelligence official who confirmed the plan to CBS News called the threat "credible" and said it came from the same al Qaeda unit that was behind the group's attempted bombing of a UPS plane, with bombs hidden inside printer toner cartridges, in October 2010.[9] "We're aware that terrorists have been interested in doing this kind of thing for a long time," a U.S. official told CNN, of the poisoning plots.[10] A raid of an al Qaeda cell in London in 2003 turned up quantities of ricin.[11]

So why would someone like Omar Khadr – who, according to the contemporary media portrayals, was merely a dutiful son taking up arms in Afghanistan to defend Muslim lands from invading foreigners – need to learn about such things as poisons and assassinations, unless he were training to become an international terrorist – another Khalid Sheikh Mohammed or Osama bin Laden? Of course, al Qaeda has been big into assassinations, far outside Afghanistan, for years too: in 2003, al Qaeda agents assassinated U.S. diplomat Laurence Foley outside his home in Amman, Jordan. That same year, it bombed a United Nations building in Iraq, killing the special UN envoy, Sérgio Vieira de Mello.[12] Mustafa Abu al-Yazid, an al Qaeda commander in Afghanistan, was the man who claimed responsibility for organizing, with the Khadrs' close family friend Ayman al-Zawahiri, the assassination of former Pakistani prime minister Benazir Bhutto in Rawalpindi, Pakistan, in 2007.[13] Intelligence has uncovered al Qaeda plots in the past to assassinate former U.S. president Bill Clinton, Pope John Paul II, former Philippine president Fidel Ramos, and Indonesian president Megawati Sukarnoputri.[14]

Khadr was training to become a serious terrorist leader – the James Bond of jihad. This was someone who already, at his age, knew "where he could get false documentation to travel around Afghanistan," as one doctor who interviewed Khadr reported.[15] He was, as that same expert noted in observing a videotape the U.S. military recovered in Afghanistan that showed Khadr helping to build landmines, assembling high-powered, deadly explosives virtually unsupervised while his fellow terrorists milled around in the same room. He was evidently expert enough in his explosives training for them to trust him to build bombs powerful enough to overturn an armoured vehicle without worrying that he might inadvertently blow them all up instead.[16] And when he tossed a grenade at American troops that day at the al Qaeda compound in Khost, he was, as the expert pointed out, "deadly accurate."[17]

He trained in martial arts. He had studied so he was fluent or conversational in five languages, according to his confession (even Agent 007 could speak only four, according to the James Bond Wikipedia entry). Omar Khadr surely must have been eager to become expert in all the various ways he could wreak terror, not just in Afghanistan, but back home in Toronto, or in the United States. Poisons and assassinations are the kind of thing you need to know for killing infidels where they live, not for fighting U.S. soldiers in Afghanistan. And Khadr confessed to working with al Qaeda cleric Sheikh Issa bin Zayed Al Nayhan, who "taught a class" in the Koranic way of terror. One lesson, Khadr revealed, was that "Americans were non-believers and it was justified to kill them" anywhere. He told U.S. officials that after his training, he "considered himself to be an active member of al Qaeda and he shared the same goals as the organization, which are to target and kill all Americans, whether civilian or military, anywhere they can be found and to 'plunder their money.'"

So privileged and elite was Khadr's al Qaeda education that he "attended one-on-one private terrorist training," he said, even though he admitted he knew full well "that such training was wrongful." It was, he said, "to be used in attacks against the Jews because the Jews are always fighting, which suggested . . . that someone Jewish should be killed."

Israel, of course, didn't have any soldiers in Afghanistan. And however many Jewish soldiers might be counted among the NATO forces there, they must surely be a tiny minority. In fact, while it's probably fair to say that Jews are likely overrepresented relative to their numbers in the population in some vocations (probably accounting and law, to name just a couple), they don't tend to have a reputation these days for flocking in large numbers to join the military. Anyway, the idea that "Jews are always fighting" sounds pretty odd coming from a guy whose family effectively championed the armed struggle of Muslims – Khadr maintained in his confession that "every Muslim in the world should fight the non-believers" as long as "non-believers" had a presence in a Muslim country, even if it was a peaceful presence, as with American bases in Kuwait and Saudi Arabia – and whose own co-religionists in Africa and the Middle East are probably responsible for more of the world's fighting than the Jews could ever be fairly accused of. But then, Khadr had a knack for absolving himself of the very offences that he claimed justified his hunting down of Jews and Christians. In his confession, he stated that "every country should worry about one's own country and not interfere in other countries' problems," which sounds halfway reasonable, unless you notice the fact that Omar Khadr was a Canadian citizen, out to murder Americans, in the middle of Afghanistan.

Where else Omar Khadr was planning to use his elite terrorist training skills is something that, thankfully, we can now only imagine. As a devotee of Osama bin Laden and Ayman al-Zawahiri, and as someone committed to sharing the goals of al Qaeda, he was clearly ready to promote the killing of "all Americans, whether civilian or military, anywhere they can be found."[18] Back in Toronto, his family came out to court hearings for the so-called Toronto 18, the Islamist terrorists arrested in Canada for a plot to assassinate the prime minister and bomb several strategic sites in downtown Toronto.[19] (The Khadrs attended the same Middle East–funded mosque – "a focal point for Toronto area Islamic radicals," as the RCMP described it – as members of the Toronto 18 terrorist cell.[20])

Khadr was determined to kill Jews, and we know he wouldn't be likely to find them in Afghanistan or Pakistan. He was training in poisons and assassinations. He was a pro with explosives. He had learned how to spy, to calculate troop movements and plan attacks on them, to sabotage, to select targets. He was becoming an expert in multiple languages. He is "advantaged by worldly sophistication and language skills," according to one of his most thorough psychiatric reports.[21] He was learning the Koranic rules about killing infidels. He had developed "intimate knowledge of the al Qaeda organization and its goals."[22] He wanted to "plunder" the money of the infidels. He had amassed the skills for being a communicator, a human resources manager, a logistics coordinator, an intelligence expert: Omar Khadr was the prince of al Qaeda, grooming himself to become an Islamist crime boss like his father. More likely, much like Michael Corleone, his ambition was to become an even bigger, more brutal Godfather than his dad.

"He is absolutely more seasoned than the other al Qaeda fighters," noted one Guantanamo Bay interrogator.[23] This was someone who, still in his teens, was already more lethal and war-ready than almost anyone else at a prison filled with hundreds of terrorists. More so, maybe, than even the American soldiers guarding him: that's what an expert psychiatrist analyzing Khadr concluded. "Omar Khadr was not some snot-nosed fifteen year old," wrote Dr. Michael Welner in his forensic psychiatric study of Khadr, developed after interviewing Khadr for two days. It's one reason, he believed, that Khadr was able to outsmart so many of the interrogation methods the U.S. investigators had used on him. Khadr, Dr. Welner wrote, "had whirled around far more than his interrogators. What is to be spooked by some foul military interrogators with ugly tattoos," when Khadr had been around so much worse – when he lived and breathed among the worst and most senior killers that al Qaeda had to offer?[24]

Omar Khadr plainly had a passion for three things: mayhem, murder, and money. In his confession, he admitted that a key motivation for him wasn't just plundering Americans' money but also the $1,500 bounty that al Qaeda had put on the head of any American killed. Fifteen hundred dollars is a decent amount of money, but it's not exactly a fortune: the average college-aged teenager might earn about that much in three or four weeks working at Starbucks, or mowing lawns over the summer. But for Omar Khadr, that kind of regular work clearly wasn't worth doing for that kind of cash. Murdering a human being, on the other hand, violently taking someone's life and destroying their families, robbing their children of a parent – as Khadr did to Christopher Speer's two little children, Tanner and Taryn Speer – that, as Omar Khadr evidently saw it, was a fair way to earn some walking-around dough.

How much cheaper can someone's estimation of a breathing, loving human life get? Even mafia hit men must charge more than $1,500 to rub someone out. Omar Khadr is plainly a man without conscience or morals – at least when it came to earning a few bucks. To almost every human being on the planet, taking a life would be a very difficult thing to do, probably the most difficult thing you could ask of someone. For Khadr, it apparently looked easier, and more attractive, than serving cappuccinos or pushing a lawn mower around. How ironic that the United States, the very country that has been accused of acting immorally, and callously, in its treatment of Omar Khadr, was willing to spend hundreds of thousands of dollars on saving his life that day in Afghanistan: to save just a single one of his eyes that had been damaged by shrapnel while he was attacking American troops, the U.S. army specially flew in an ophthalmologist to the army hospital to operate on him. And the United States has spent hundreds of thousands more keeping him well fed at Guantanamo (he had all kinds of special dietary demands, including the need for "a side of cheese and olives every meal" and "a side of olive oil with lunch"[25]) as well as offering him even more medical treatment while in custody: X-rays, arthroscopic surgery, and physiotherapy to alleviate some leg discomfort that Khadr had complained about.[26] This for a man who thinks a life is worth no more than $1,500.

It's impossible to read Omar Khadr's confession to the court and consider this gangster anything like the child soldier his supporters claim him to be, as if he were somehow a vulnerable boy forced to take up arms. Child soldiers are terribly abused: they are virtual slaves, compelled under duress to do things they could never otherwise imagine themselves doing, and desperate to escape. When the Nazis press-ganged high school students into Hitler's army in the desperate dying days of the Third Reich, "most often the dazed and frightened teen-agers surrendered in tears without firing a shot."[27] Like Khadr, they may have grown up in a culture that inculcated them to believe that killing was acceptable; unlike Khadr, they did not embrace slaughter with relish. Omar Khadr didn't see himself as a child soldier; "he considered himself a terrorist," according to his confession.

Like some degenerate Agent 007, he gave himself a licence to kill Americans and Jews.

In his confession, Khadr talks about how he "hoped" to cause "destruction" with his bombs. He "voluntarily chose to construct and plant" the IEDs designed to destroy human life in a most violent way "in support of al Qaeda and to further the aims of the organization." In a videotape recovered at the compound where Khadr had been holed up with his al Qaeda comrades, Khadr is shown building landmines and "excitedly looking forward to killing Americans"; he was "smiling, enthusiastic, and [had a] relaxed attitude" forensic psychiatrist Dr. Michael Welner was careful to note.[28] Khadr was a zealous recruit, eager to distinguish himself as the most vicious of all. He sought to "maximize the opportunity for death and destruction."[29] He was "proudest" when planning his deadly attacks. According to his confession, "during an interview in October 2002, Khadr stated he felt happy when he heard that he had killed an American." When he was in U.S. custody, "he would recall his killing of the U.S. soldier and it would make him feel good."

He would "feel good." Think about that. That is not only the exact opposite response you'd expect from a traumatized child soldier, forced to witness, and participate in, a nightmare of horrors. In fact, it would be a strange reaction coming from nearly any soldier, even a grizzled veteran. Killing people is just not the kind of thing that brings a normal person a feeling of joy or consoles them when they're feeling blue. Normal people simply don't feel "proudest" about their work in tearing human beings apart with deadly explosives. Police officers don't reminisce fondly about the criminals they've had to gun down; actually, they usually take years of therapy to deal with it, if they ever do get over it. Khadr, meanwhile, showed no signs of post-traumatic stress disorder, not even trouble with sleeping or nightmares, as psychiatrists who reviewed his case pointed out.[30] He slept just fine. Lacking any sense of guilt or conscience, taking pleasure in killing another human being as Omar Khadr obviously does? That's just psychopathic.

Consider Khadr's behaviour that July day in Khost, the day he threw the grenade that would kill Christopher Speer, and when his terrorist gang attacked Sgt. Layne Morris, leaving him blind in one eye. This must have been the moment that Khadr had chosen to set himself apart as a future al Qaeda leader. He and his comrades had settled in an al Qaeda compound, but when they heard news that the Americans were coming, the owner of the compound himself fled. It's important to pay attention to that detail because that was always an option for Khadr too – just retreating, instead of engaging U.S. soldiers. From the moment he arrived at the compound until the moment of his capture, he had that option. He had arrived planning to do some translating work and "did not have to stay," as he explained to one interrogator. But when he learned "that they were planning to kill Americans, he decided to stay" – he was free to go but leapt at the chance to spill some infidel blood.[31] And once the Americans arrived, they "asked the occupants, including Khadr, to come outside and talk" to them. The request came in both English and Pashto: both were languages in which Khadr was fluent.

But Khadr refused. He wasn't ambushed or caught off guard. He didn't even have to be there. Yet his response to an offer of peaceful surrender was to pick up an AK-47, put on an ammunition vest, and hunker down for a fight.[32] When the Americans sent a pair of Afghani translators to approach the compound and ask "for the occupants to come out," Khadr and his fellow cell members shot them both in the head, killing them. They weren't Jews or Americans: they were just people in Omar Khadr's way. They needed to die.

During the firefight that followed, Khadr admitted that "U.S. forces gave the occupants inside the compound multiple chances to surrender. At one point, the women and the children in the compound exited the compound and U.S. forces escorted them to safety." But Omar Khadr didn't consider himself one of the children in the compound, unlike his fans in the mainstream press. He considered himself an al Qaeda warrior and was determined to vanquish the American infidels. We now know that there was nothing that he wanted more desperately than that. And, heck, at $1,500 for every corpse he could create, he might even make some money while he was at it.

He "decided to fight the U.S. forces rather than surrender or exit the compound peacefully,"[33] he admitted. He didn't do it because he had to, because he was being compelled to, at risk of being punished by his terrorist comrades. Quite the contrary, as he admitted in his confession he "understood, at the time of the firefight, that he would not have faced any repercussions from the other members of the al Qaeda cell if he would have chosen not to fight and surrendered with the women and children to U.S. forces" – he had already been injured by shrapnel from a nearby grenade. He "could have left the compound if he wanted," he confessed. But Khadr surely imagined himself to be a special kind of al Qaeda fighter. An elite fighter. A born leader. An al Qaeda Idol. And so, ready to make his stand, to show what he was made of, Omar Khadr "chose to stay behind and fight the Americans."

And after it was all over, when the compound had been nearly obliterated and the American soldiers, including medic Christopher Speer, were finally able to enter, Omar Khadr was the only one of the al Qaeda fighters still alive. This was likely no coincidence, reported Dr. Welner, the psychiatrist who examined Khadr: this was a highly trained, extremely keen terrorist who knew how to fight, kill, and live to fight again. "The defendant emerged alive from a compound that was decimated to the end that all the dead could not even be found for all of the rubble . . . it was his training that saved him."[34] Khadr confessed that he knew the Americans weren't coming to kill him; he "thought that the soldiers entering the compound were looking for wounded or dead and that the firefight was over."[35] He "was not under the impression that U.S. soldiers were preparing to charge his position, attack or engage him." He knew that all his comrades were dead

48

and that the Americans were coming only to find, and help, anyone who had been injured – people like him. Yet he had saved his ammunition, his grenades, as any smart soldier does, waiting for the perfect moment to attack, to cause maximum destruction.

He didn't drop his weapons and surrender peacefully. That kind of thing simply wouldn't befit the prince of al Qaeda. In his mind, Khadr must have imagined that this was when his legend would be born: he would single-handedly defeat this squad of Americans. He had a gun and a store of grenades ready that he could use to take them all on. As he himself confessed, he positioned himself "behind a crumbling wall, armed and threw a Russian F-1 grenade." He "threw the grenade with the specific intent of killing or injuring as many Americans as he could." That grenade would explode into the brain of Christopher Speer and eventually kill him.

And thinking of that terrible, brutal, bloody act – hiding, lurking, waiting, and ambushing an American medic – that is what makes Omar Khadr feel "happy." That is what makes him "feel good."

CHAPTER 4

WHOM DID KHADR MURDER?

"Omar Khadr is not a child soldier in the manner that has afflicted so many conflicts. He was never uprooted from his family, never desensitized to violence with drugs and alcohol, never groomed into violence from a peaceful origin. He glorified violence rather than was horrified by it (as are child soldiers). Khadr was a worldly 15-year-old rather than a naïve one. His family supported his violence, rather than adopting it from captors' influence. Child soldiers seek nothing. Omar Khadr sought martyrdom."

Dr. Michael Welner, April 14, 2011

S oldiers killed in action are almost always called "heroes" in their home countries. And to a certain extent it's almost always true. While the men and women in uniform aren't there entirely unselfishly – many love the thrill and adventure of serving abroad – the word *hero* comes from the Greek word *heros*, which literally means protector or defender. More to the point, there is something unquestionably heroic about doing what others will not do, even if you happen to enjoy doing it: leaving your family and loved ones behind for months at a time to face death in some foreign land all in the name of serving your nation's interests is pretty heroic. In a volunteer army like America's or Canada's, soldiers sign up fully aware of the fact that they could easily die on the job, and yet, they sign up just the same.

The most dangerous job in Canada, by fatality, is probably fishing and trapping, which, in 2004, recorded a rate of 52 deaths per 100,000 workers, followed closely by mining, quarrying, and oil well work, with 50 deaths per 100,000 employees. Third was logging and forestry, with 33 deaths per 100,000 workers.[1]

Canadian troops began their major deployment in Afghanistan in January 2002. As of January 2011, nine years later, 154 troops had been killed there[2] out of about 35,000 who have served there.[3] That works out to 440 deaths per 100,000 soldiers. Spread out over nine years, that's 49 deaths per 100,000, meaning a tour of duty in Kandahar now ranks as one of the most deadly jobs any Canadian can do.

Unlike some fishermen and trappers, or miners and quarry workers, soldiers don't usually take the job because it happens to be one of the few things on offer in their local economy. The men and women who populate Canada's military casualty list, for instance, just as frequently come from economically diversified places like Montreal and Chicoutimi, Sudbury and Toronto, Edmonton and Calgary, or Saskatoon. They didn't enlist to fight in Afghanistan because they had no other options. Facing the daunting danger of fighting for Canada in Afghanistan was their choice.

Still, of all the heroes who risked their skin for some higher calling than materialism, some stand out especially tall.

U.S. Sgt. 1st Class Christopher Speer was not the sort of forceful, cocky type of fellow you might imagine would become a member of Delta Force. Delta is the U.S. army's storied elite counter-terrorist unit. Its legend and exploits have been so lionized that there have been numerous books about Deltas. Also movies. Even video games. These are the guys who know how to rappel out of helicopters onto rooftops of buildings full of heavily armed bad guys. The force's creator,

Col. Charlie Beckwith, designed Delta to be an antidote to the "mechanization and bureaucratization of modern warfare." He imagined, as the *Atlantic* once described it, a company of spirited men who, like Beckwith, were "impatient with rank, rules, and politics, focused entirely on mission . . . not just good, they were magnificent."[4] Delta Force was sent in to free the fifty-three Americans held hostage by Islamic revolutionaries in Iran, a failed mission, and to capture Somali warlord Gen. Mohamed Ali Farrah Aidid, a terrible botch-up captured in the book and movie *Black Hawk Down*. But it also succeeded in apprehending Panamanian strongman Manuel Noriega and played critical roles in the Persian Gulf War and the invasion of Afghanistan. The 1986 action film *The Delta Force* portrayed the soldiers in a fictional rescue of a plane full of Americans from Lebanese terrorists. It starred Chuck Norris and Lee Marvin. The CBS TV show *The Unit* was based on Delta Force exploits. If you watch the news, the Delta guy is the one "always in a bad place, and the Delta Force member is the man who looks like he's at home," wrote Eric Haney, a Delta alumnus and author of *Inside Delta Force*.[5]

But Christopher Speer was no brawny, take-no-prisoners bull of a man like Chuck Norris, with a cigar clenched in his teeth and biceps bulging out of a sleeveless T-shirt. His route to becoming one of the youngest members of Fort Bragg's elite counter-terrorism unit was an old-fashioned one: he was just, by all accounts, a fine, smart, and unflinching soldier.

Speer had joined the army because he hoped to become a doctor; as a medic, he'd get on-the-job training, and then, eventually, his medical school paid for. He was quiet; he was a passionate Elvis fan; he liked to sketch.[6]

Christopher Speer was an exceptional soldier, but not because of his fierceness or aggression, the kinds of qualities often held up in popular culture as the essence of an elite warrior. In fact, Speer impressed his comrades and his superiors for exhibiting starkly different qualities – though none any less the makings of an honourable army man. The army captain who eulogized Christopher Speer at his funeral spoke about how those soldiers who knew Speer were so struck by his "good nature, his sense of serenity, the feeling that Chris had made peace with the world and that maybe he had found some answers that the rest of us were still looking for."[7]

Christopher Speer was an adoring family man. When he shipped out for Afghanistan in July 2002, he left behind a three-year-old daughter, Taryn – after telling her he was going to the desert she excitedly exclaimed, "You'll be riding camels!"[8] – and a nine-month-old boy, Tanner. It was his habit to leave love notes around the house for his wife, Tabitha, and children to find; when he left for Afghanistan, his family would continue to discover the messages secreted around their home months after he was killed. When he died, five of his organs were donated to needy patients. "Christopher constantly put the needs of others before his own," Tabitha said.

"Christopher continued to help others with life through his death."[9]

Speer wasn't in Afghanistan very long. He left his family behind in North Carolina on July 13, 2002; he met Omar Khadr's grenade on July 27. He only had a chance to speak to his wife once while he was there. But in just two weeks, Christopher Speer accomplished more, demonstrated more of a commitment to helping the helpless, than most soldiers would have the opportunity, or perhaps even the capability, to do. Just days before he was killed, Speer came upon a pair of Afghan children stranded in a minefield. One of them had been injured after detonating an explosive. Speer ran through the deadly obstacle course to rescue them. He treated them on the scene, flagged down a passing ambulance, and stayed with them after one hospital refused to treat them until he could get them into a clinic run by Spanish doctors that were willing to take them in.[10] By all accounts, thanks to Christopher Speer, those kids survived.

A man named Tim Rivera from Powder Springs, Georgia, years ago set up a website called Fallen Heroes of Operation Enduring Freedom. It is sort of an online memorial to all the American men and women killed in the war in Afghanistan, listing their names, where they hailed from, their unit, their age, and how they died. It also features a place where people can post tributes to the soldiers they knew, or even to those they didn't. When Christopher Speer's name was posted on this site after he died from his injuries on August 7, 2002, people who hadn't talked to him or seen him for years began sharing their memories of him. They all paint the same portrait: of a kind, respectful, honourable, helpful, and brave man.

Adam Wirth of Beaver Island, Michigan, remembered they were on the same team together in Special Forces school. "He was a hell of a good man," he wrote. "Quiet spoken, serious about his training and always there taking care of the team." Lon Hill from Kemah, Texas, was Speer's roommate at army training, before Speer left for Special Forces training. "He was a stand up guy," he wrote. "His death is a huge loss to this country." Christopher Vedvick, in Fort Bragg, North Carolina, knew Speer "only in passing," while they were in Afghanistan, he said. But they saw action together, and he wrote, "I knew enough to have respect for the man. I only know that he was brave enough to step up to the fight after me and my fire team were wounded in a fire fight with the enemy."

Jarrod Gonzales went to high school with Speer in New Mexico. "The thing I remember most about him was his sense of humor. He could look at you with a straight face and tell the funniest jokes," he said. "There was always a certain element to his personality that told you he was a strong individual." Barry Hugo from Bay City, Michigan, was at army war college with Chris Speer too. "He was the best soldier I had the opportunity to know, always squared away, always helping others and always trying to do better," he wrote. "He was a tall, strong and honest person, full of love and hope. I will always remember our time in Pennsylvania." He named his son Christopher, he said, after his dear friend Chris Speer. "I feel compelled to let everyone know that."

Read post after post after post and two things strike you: one, Speer left a deep impression on so many people he met, an impression that stayed with them for years after he left them – an impression of an exceptionally decent individual. The other thing may be the number of Canadians who signed up to pay their respects to Christopher Speer: from Ontario, British Columbia, Alberta, and Prince Edward Island. As one Canadian wrote:

> While it's not said nearly often enough, many many Canadians also recognize the selfless sacrifice people like Chris Speer make for others. Reading his story gives hope that through the politics and posturing that goes along with armed conflict, there are caring and compassionate people like Chris out there doing their best to help others in need. The press and the media don't speak for the Canadian public when they characterize the offender responsible for Chris' death. I feel it's important for Chris' family to know that there are Canadians out here who can set aside the politics and grandstanding that surrounds the trial of his assailant, and recognize that the story of the person who we lost that day, and the selfless work he did, does not fall on deaf eyes and ears.

Of course the most difficult tribute of all to read on Tim Rivera's site was put there by Tabitha Lee Speer, Christopher's widow:

> I was given the honor of not only knowing Chris, I spent the happiest years of my life with him. We married and had two beautiful children. Chris made all my dreams come true, it was as though he completed me. It has been two years and seven months since his death and I still find it hard to believe that he won't be coming home. Our Daughter is now almost six, she talks about her Daddy constantly, our Son who is three has so much trouble understanding why his Daddy won't be coming home! He asks for his Daddy daily, can he see me? Does he hear me? Can he hold my hand if I reach up to Heaven? Will he come home after he's done in Heaven? My Daughter and I do our best to answer his questions.
>
> We miss you so much and love you more than any words could ever possibly express. I can see you in their faces, with each and every smile and silly little smirk. You are so alive in them both, it amazes me! We have a little three year old version of you, he becomes more and more like you every day. They both have your sense of humor and are always smiling.
>
> We love you, you are our true HERO!
>
> I Love You Today, Tomorrow and Forever!

The public hasn't heard much from Tabitha Speer since her husband was murdered. In part, that was

Tabitha's choice; she kept a low profile, likely too devastated by her loss and too focused on caring for her kids to want to be a public figure. In part, though, it was the media's decision. Persistent reporters willing to work hard enough can usually get the interview they want, even with someone reluctant to talk. But most reporters just didn't want to talk about Tabitha Speer. No doubt a lot of them felt uncomfortable hounding a young widow with two children for an interview. That's understandable. But a lot of journalists also wanted to pretend that Tabitha Speer didn't exist, that Christopher Speer didn't exist. They would mention his name in their stories, sure, the same way they might mention the name of a lawyer or a politician who played a role in their news story. They almost never mention his wife and kids. They wanted most of all to talk about Omar Khadr.

Usually when reporters write about murder, they emphasize the victim's story. They interview surviving family members and friends. They paint a portrait of the lives that were shattered. After 9/11, *The New York Times* ran a "Portraits of Grief" series, featuring a short profile, a "snapshot of each victim's personality, of a life lived," for every single victim killed in the attacks.[11] It took nearly four months to get through them all, but get through them all they did. These stories were important.

In Omar Khadr's case, though, the Speers complicate the story. Without them, Omar Khadr is a victim, a naïf, a youngster caught up in the maw of the great American war machine, exploited, mistreated, abused, and unjustly detained. A "victim" of America's flawed War on Terror, as the *Toronto Star*'s Michelle Shephard summed it up. A murdered twenty-eight-year-old medic of uncommon respectability, a shattered family, the heartbreaking story of real, genuine victims – people who, unlike Omar Khadr, had done nothing at all wrong yet suffered terrible pain and loss? That just clouds the narrative. Want proof? A search through the Canadian Infomart database of news stories from the nearly ten years since that fateful day in Khost, Afghanistan, turns up 1,181 mentions of the name "Christopher Speer"; just 219 mentions of "Tabitha Speer." And stories starring the terrorist Omar Khadr? 12,409.

Thankfully, the lawyers prosecuting Omar Khadr at Guantanamo didn't forget that. They went in to fight a trial over the murder of a man, and the consequences of that. They tabled as evidence letters written by Christopher Speer's children after he was murdered.[12] In one, an eleven-year-old Taryn Speer writes to Omar Khadr: "I'm mad at you for what you did to my family. Because of you my dad never got to see me play soccer or see me go to kindergarten. You make me really sad and mad at you because of that." Tanner Speer, the son who never knew his dad, wrote this: "I think that Omhar Kader should go to jail for [redacted] years because of the open hole he made in my family and killing my dad. Now because of Omhar Kader I praticly never new or seen my dad and I don't have a memory of my dad." He finished his essay in a flourish, writing in large block letters: "ARMY ROCK'S!! BAD GUYS STINK!!"

The child gets it. He knows Khadr's bad. That he's ripped people's lives apart. That he belongs in prison for what he did.

It's hard to believe that such an elementary understanding still eludes so many grown-ups.

CHAPTER 5

WHAT IS A CHILD SOLDIER?

*"The bearing of Ahmed Khadr was not so much that
Omar Khadr was powerless to resist that authority. . .
Omar Khadr had options about how far he had to go for
his father. An apt pupil, it was Omar Khadr delighting on
videotape, far from his father, in the prospect of killing
Americans."*

Dr. Michael Welner, forensic psychiatric
analysis of Omar Khadr, July 5, 2010

63

There has never been any real doubt that Omar Khadr is a terrorist. He grew up in Canada's self-described al Qaeda family and he was captured in a firefight with U.S. troops in Afghanistan – along with home movies showing him with a machine gun and assembling bombs. The main defence put forward by Khadr's advocates was not that he didn't commit horrible violence. It's that he was just a child, and so no matter what he had actually done, it was illegal for the United States to jail and prosecute him, and for Canada to go along with that.

Professor David Crane[1] is one such apologist. He's a professor at the College of Law at Syracuse University, but more importantly he was the prosecutor of war criminals in the strife-torn African country of Sierra Leone. Crane runs a website called Impunity Watch, which focuses on bringing war criminals to justice. Which is ironic, given his views on Khadr.

Crane was invited to testify before Canada's parliamentary foreign affairs committee looking into the matter of Khadr's detention. He was as clear as one could be: Khadr was not guilty of war crimes because no one under eighteen could ever be guilty of war crimes. In Sierra Leone, said Crane, "I realized that no child has what we call the *mens rea*, the evil-thinking mind, to commit a war crime." In his time in Africa, he simply decided never to prosecute a minor, no matter what they had done. "I chose not to, even up to the age of 18," he said. "Even if they voluntarily join the [military] force, they're really not voluntarily joining the force."

It's possible to understand Crane's thinking. His experience with child soldiers in Sierra Leone was terrifying: children as young as eight or nine forced at gunpoint to join paramilitary squads, brainwashed and drugged, and completely at the mercy of the gang leaders who were exploiting them. Crane's testimony began with one such anecdote – a twelve-year-old boy who approached Crane one day and said he had been with a group of other children who were captured by a Sierra Leone terrorist group called the Revolutionary United Front. The captured children were asked whether they wanted to join, and those who said no were killed on the spot. Those who were left had RUF carved into their chests with a knife and were forced to fight.

Crane said the boy "looked me right in the eye and said he had killed people, he was sorry, he didn't mean it. He was 12, the conflict had been over about two years, so you can do the math. He probably was eight or nine years old when he was killing human beings."

During his time in Africa, Crane had many emotional encounters like that with child soldiers: "I have looked them in the eye, I have talked to them, I have hugged them, I've cried with them," he said.

It is truly heart-breaking. But compare that use of the phrase *child soldier* with Omar Khadr. Khadr was a few weeks shy of his sixteenth birthday – not an eight- or nine-year-old boy who should have been in Grade 3. Khadr enthusiastically embraced the family business of terror – no one had to threaten him with death if he didn't participate. Khadr didn't need to be physically branded like an animal and jacked up on drugs to comply. And in the final battle in Afghanistan, Khadr was not forced to fight under duress. On the contrary, he insisted on staying to fight, even after others fled their position when Americans offered a ceasefire.

The young children referred to by Crane were genuinely terrified and were obviously innocent tools abused by evil men. It's possible to come to Crane's conclusion about child soldiers in Sierra Leone – that they never really were the ones to blame. How different they were, though, from Khadr – not a child, but about to turn sixteen; not forced to participate, but gleeful to do so; and not regretful in the least – but more committed to jihad than ever. Crane said he never prosecuted a minor because he never believed they had the requisite *mens rea* – the "guilty mind" required to convict a criminal. Omar Khadr is the dictionary definition of *mens rea*.

Of course, the younger the person, the less likely they're criminally responsible for their actions. But even Canada's Youth Criminal Justice Act, brought in by the Liberals in 2003 to replace the Young Offenders Act, acknowledges that children as young as twelve can be held to account for their crimes, and serious youth criminals, such as murderers and rapists, can be sentenced to adult-length sentences.

In 2006, a twelve-year-old girl from Medicine Hat, Alberta, killed her parents and younger brother. She was charged and convicted of three counts of third-degree murder, and given a ten-year sentence. Pretending that teenagers (or even occasional twelve-year-olds) aren't responsible for their actions would be laughable to any store owner who has been shoplifted or any homeowner whose property has been vandalized. But it takes a really clever professor to claim that teenaged murderers shouldn't be prosecuted.

Crane wasn't the only advocate to whitewash Khadr of any responsibility for his actions. So did Roméo Dallaire, the former Canadian Forces general who served on a peacekeeping mission in Rwanda and who is now a Liberal Senator. Dallaire testified to the parliamentary committee about Khadr, and he went much further than Cranc did.

"Omar Khadr is a victim, not a terrorist or a perpetrator," he declared. But Dallaire didn't just sanctify the al Qaeda fighter. He denounced the United States and discredited the integrity of its legal and human rights. To Dallaire, Khadr is "a child soldier, prosecuted in a foreign land, on an illegal charge, by an illegal court."

Dallaire was just getting warmed up. He said that by prosecuting Khadr, the United States "is doing exactly what the extremists and terrorists are doing." He said the

United States turned themselves into a "police state," and is "no better than the other gang."

Jason Kenney, the Conservative cabinet minister who sat on the committee the day Dallaire testified, challenged Dallaire's comparison between the United States and al Qaeda. But Dallaire didn't back down from that statement: "If you want it in black and white, then I'm only too prepared to give it to you: absolutely," he said. It was a shocking thing to hear from a former high-ranking officer in the Canadian military.

Of course, not all of the legal criticisms of Khadr's arrest, detention, and prosecution were based merely on anti-Americanism or the naive declaration that no one under eighteen could be held responsible for a crime.

The Khadr lobby argued that a United Nations treaty called the Convention on the Rights of the Child was being violated by the prosecution of Khadr and that the trial at Guantanamo Bay was illegal too.

Ironically, when Khadr's own lawyer, Lt. Cdr. William Kuebler, testified before Parliament, he confirmed that the prosecution of Khadr was in fact legal.

When Kuebler testified in Ottawa on April 29, 2008, he was a passionate advocate for his client – denying that Khadr killed Sergeant Speer, blaming Khadr's parents for his radicalism, and calling for Canada to repatriate him. It was unseemly to see Kuebler – a U.S. naval officer – spin Khadr's terrorist jihad as some sort of self-defence. "Even if he did everything that the U.S. government said he did, what he is guilty of, at worst, is throwing a hand grenade as a soldier in a firefight against people who were trying to kill him," Kuebler told the MPs. But despite such personal loyalty to Khadr, Kuebler did concede that the prosecution of him didn't violate international law.

Kuebler had the honesty to concede that "Khadr is not the stereotypical child soldier, like those from Sierra Leone," and that he was certainly not the only "child soldier" in Guantanamo Bay. Most importantly, Kuebler acknowledged that the UN Convention on the Rights of the Child acknowledged that just because a soldier was fifteen, sixteen, or seventeen didn't mean they weren't a soldier and didn't prevent their prosecutions. (Before the committee, Dallaire himself acknowledged that the Canadian Forces recruit soldiers who are sixteen and seventeen.)

Kuebler's testimony also rebutted Dallaire's outrageous claim that the United States was an illegal police state. He noted that the special military prosecutions of terrorists that began after 9/11 had been struck down by the U.S. Supreme Court twice – but that the process Khadr was prosecuted under was a revised system that was rewritten to comply with the law.

But as American constitutional expert Howard Anglin told the parliamentary committee,[2] the biggest error made by Khadr's lobbyists was that they simply didn't understand how to apply laws to battlefields. "Most critics" of Guantanamo Bay, said Anglin, "will accept nothing less than the full protections of a civilian criminal court, even for unlawful combatants captured on the battlefield, and they denounce anything short of those protections as lawless."

The kind of legal process required to handle terrorists captured in wars is obviously going to be different than what ordinary criminal lawyers come to expect in Canada. "Many witnesses are dead, there's no forensic detective squad to document the scene, and most of the surviving witnesses are serving overseas at the time of trial. For all these reasons, military commissions throughout history have not applied the same evidentiary standards we demand of a civilian criminal trial. If they were required to do so, it would be virtually impossible to ever try detainees," said Anglin.

For this reason, noted Anglin, the world's civilized countries signed a series of treaties called the Geneva Conventions to set out the basic laws governing battlefields, including the treatment of prisoners.

Trials of wartime crimes allow hearsay evidence and allow prosecutors to withhold sensitive information that would reveal military secrets. Wartime rules also allow government to suspend habeas corpus, the ancient Latin phrase meaning the right not to be detained indefinitely without a hearing – one of the most bitter complaints made by Khadr's allies. As Anglin cheekily pointed out to the committee, "Prime Minister Trudeau suspended habeas corpus during the October Crisis in 1970. Indeed, Trudeau sent tanks into the streets of Montreal and rounded up hundreds of Canadian citizens and detained them without charge for weeks over the kidnapping of two persons and the death of one. We can only be thankful that the full devastation of 9/11 did not take place on Trudeau's watch."

Trudeau suspended habeas corpus for Canadian citizens, within Canada. But the Geneva Conventions – which date back to the 1860s – permit enemy soldiers to be detained without a trial until the war is over.

Article 4 of the Third Geneva Convention, ratified in 1949, has a clear definition of a lawful combatant, and Khadr doesn't meet it. Article 4 is pretty liberal; it gives rights not only to soldiers in national armies but also to "militias and members of other volunteer corps" and "organized resistance movements," even those "operating . . . outside their own territory, even if this territory is occupied." But even guerillas have to follow certain basic rules of conduct to distinguish them from mere murderers and terrorists. They must be part of a chain of command; show a flag or emblem "recognizable at a distance"; carry their arms "openly"; and generally follow the "laws and customs of war." Khadr meets none of these criteria. He's a terrorist – not a gentleman soldier protected by the Geneva Conventions.

Omar Khadr wasn't too young to be prosecuted under the UN Convention on the Rights of the Child. That law permits prosecutions for teenagers aged fifteen and up. Guantanamo Bay isn't an illegal prison or court. The U.S. Supreme Court has considered no fewer than four challenges to it, and it operates today under revised legal procedures as laid out by the courts.

Khadr's defenders knew they couldn't win based on the facts of the case – facts Khadr eventually confessed to in great detail. So they tried to smear America's basic sovereign rights to prosecute terrorists. In the end, like everything about the Khadr family, that really was the plan: to weaken the defences of the West, to undermine the moral authority of liberal democracies, to attack and discredit the military and security forces protecting the West, and to turn public opinion against both the troops and the War on Terror.

Omar Khadr was convicted. But the damage done by David Crane, Roméo Dallaire, and countless other activists and lawyers continues.

CHAPTER 6

THE RIGHTS AND RESPONSIBILITIES OF BEING CANADIAN

"Omar Khadr is an enemy belligerent because he has purposefully and materially supported hostilities against the United States and its coalition partners."

Confession of Omar Ahmed Khadr, October 13, 2010

E very Canadian knows that there are certain rights afforded to citizens of this country. It's nearly impossible to miss: the Canadian liberal media, every bit as infatuated as the national legal industry with the mixed legacy of the Charter of Rights and Freedoms, never tires of emphasizing the broad and apparently inviolable rights so many of us supposedly deserve just for having been lucky enough to have been born into one of Canada's ten provinces or three territories. In only the last few years, somewhere in the media, the "rights of citizenship" have been invoked in questioning the requirement that new citizens swear an oath to the Queen, insisting that children born outside the country to Canadian parents deserve full citizenship, making police and firefighting services an entitlement, demanding the federal government "rescue" someone banned from travel by the United States' no-fly list, and requiring the provision of socialized health care and other social programs.

When thousands of Lebanese Canadians who'd long ago returned to their motherland to make their homes and build careers in the Levant found themselves suddenly caught in a war zone during the fighting between Israel and Hezbollah in 2006, they flooded our embassy, demanding that Ottawa evacuate them at the taxpayers' expense.[1] That, they said, was a right of citizenship too – the federal government as travel agent and airline to whisk you back to the safety of Canada's bosom, no matter how long you'd been away, how tenuous your connection to Canada had become, or whether you'd ever paid a dime of Canadian taxes in your life.

Canada evacuated thousands of dual Lebanese-Canadian citizens who had made their homes in Beirut or Tyre while keeping their Canadian passports safely tucked in their back pocket should they ever need to return for a free surgery or call on Ottawa for any other services that were their "rights." Accurately dubbed by commentators as "Canadians of convenience," these nominal citizens were removed from Lebanon by the Canadian government, at no charge to them, on seven chartered cruise ships. Canada evacuated its citizens more effectively and efficiently, it turned out, than Britain or even France, which has a whole fleet of warships patrolling right there in the Mediterranean. And still they complained: the trip was "hell," groused one evacuee, because it took fifteen hours instead of seven to get to Cyprus and because of the inconvenience of being stopped by the Israeli navy, insistent on inspecting the ships to ensure they weren't hostile.[2] The ships were too hot. There was no doctor on board. There wasn't enough food. Some people had to sleep on the floor. This was a perfect portrait of the misunderstood nature of Canadian citizenship: as if the federal government is a doting parent and all of us are spoiled and petulant children demanding our "rights" to free, comfortable, first-class travel.

Few people have managed the art of manipulating and exploiting these alleged rights of Canadian citizenship better than the manipulative and exploitative Khadr family. Father Ahmed took his government-subsidized university degree and moved to Pakistan to climb the ranks of an enemy organization, returning only when he was on the run from anti-terrorist security, on terrorist fundraising junkets, or to avail himself or his family of Canada's free health care. Just before their son Ibrahim was born, the Khadrs turned up in Scarborough's Centenary Hospital; born with a heart defect, Ibrahim likely would have died had they stayed in Pakistan for the delivery. They got open-heart surgery for him at Toronto's Hospital for Sick Children, among the best pediatric institutions in the world, while Ahmed returned to Pakistan to work on his terrorist activities.

When Ibrahim was fourteen months old, Mother Maha flew back to Toronto with him so he could have another open-heart operation at the Sick Kids hospital, and so she could give birth to another son, Omar.[3] When her husband was badly injured by shrapnel wounds in 1992 in Afghanistan (only the family knows the truth about how exactly that happened), Maha flew Ahmed back to Toronto too, to get treatment at Toronto's Sunnybrook Health Sciences Centre. Pakistani doctors expected they'd have to amputate his arm and that Ahmed would never walk again; Canadian doctors, paid for by Canadian

taxpayers, saved both his arm and his legs[4] – unwittingly
ensuring that he could return to his terrorist business
in Afghanistan.

And of course the Khadrs took full advantage of their
Canadian citizenship to hector no less a VIP than the
prime minister of Canada into arranging a sweet deal for
Ahmed Khadr once he'd been arrested by Pakistani police
for his role in the 1995 Egyptian Embassy bombings. For
all this family of turncoats has cost the Canadian people,
you can be sure that Ahmed, working abroad as a terrorist
bagman, paid almost nothing back in taxes. Even today,
the Khadrs are surely taking advantage of Canadian
generosity in the ongoing medical care and support for
Kareem Khadr, left paralyzed after a firefight with police
in Pakistan.

And then there's the entire Canadian diplomatic
apparatus that has been deployed to deal with Omar
Khadr, including numerous visits by Canadian officials to
Guantanamo to look in on Omar and, as you'll read in
following chapters, lavish him with a catalogue worth of
goodies and supplies. But this, naturally, isn't enough for
Omar Khadr's fan club back in Canada. The fact that he's
been detained by the United States at all is considered an
affront to his supposed rights as a Canadian citizen, no
matter how meagre his family's connection to this country
has been all along, how much they hated it, or how
devoted they were to its destruction.

"For four years, the Liberal government did precious
little to secure Khadr's release or champion his rights as a

Canadian citizen. The Conservatives have done little more," complained Paula Simons, a columnist at the *Edmonton Journal*.[5] His lawyers have repeatedly complained that Khadr's Charter rights are being violated at Guantanamo. "The Canadian government is not prepared to stand up for Omar Khadr's rights. That should be of concern to all Canadians," chimed in Amnesty International's Canadian Secretary General, Alex Neve.[6]

But the fact is – and the law states – that being Canadian doesn't magically entitle you to diplomatic immunity in a foreign land. It doesn't give you a free pass to commit crimes anywhere you go, using your Canadian passport like a get-out-of-jail-free card from Monopoly. While diplomats who commit crimes are generally immune from being prosecuted abroad, even they still face trial at home – the general idea being that criminals are still accountable for their misdeeds, but we need to ensure that the justice meted out isn't tainted by foreign affairs intrigues. Ronald Allen Smith, every bit as much a full-fledged Canadian citizen as Omar Khadr, is sitting on death row in Montana for the 1982 murder of two people.[7] The Canadian government has actually fought to keep him there.

At any one time there are something like seventeen hundred Canadian citizens serving hard time in foreign prisons around the world.[8] The vast majority of them have no doubt done something illegal that rightfully earned them their stay there. They may be entitled to consular visits, which Khadr has received, and to check-ins from the Red Cross, which Khadr also received. But there is nothing inherently wrong with the prospect of Canadians facing justice in a foreign land just because it happens to be foreign, let alone there being some kind of right protecting us from another country's prisons should we choose to break their laws. In Canada, we may deport foreign criminals, but that typically happens only after we've delivered them the justice they deserve. Canadians wouldn't want it otherwise; to hold other countries to a different standard is puerile.

Only in jurisdictions where Canadians have legitimate reason to believe that there is an absence of reasonable justice due to corruption or political influence – as in China, Iran, North Korea, or Mexico (as in the questionable imprisonment of Canadian expatriate Brenda Martin) – do we see fit for our government to attempt to repatriate accused criminals. But the United States, Omar Khadr's jailer, hardly qualifies as a country unable to fairly dispense the rule of law; there was certainly no cry to save media baron Conrad Black from U.S. prosecution for his alleged corporate malfeasance the way there has been for Omar Khadr.

Of course, there are genuine rights guaranteed to Canadian citizens; they're itemized pretty distinctly in the Charter and in the Canadian Bill of Rights. Things like freedom of conscience and religion, security of the person, freedom of assembly and mobility and speech. We have the right to vote and to stand for office. We have a right to be protected from illegal searches; to be considered innocent, if charged with a crime, until proven guilty; and not to suffer cruel and unusual punishment. We're guaranteed equal treatment, regardless of race, age, sex, or disability.

Since the Charter received royal assent in 1982, the courts have certainly broadened the definition of some of these rights while narrowing some others (extending to prisoners the right to vote while silencing speech that might offend certain minorities), but they are fairly basic, and nowhere in either of those two documents will you find a right to a first-class evacuation from Lebanon during wartime or to free health care. As University of Toronto law professor Audrey Macklin pointed out, "The catalogue of the rights of citizenship is actually quite short."[9]

When you've left the country, that list is even shorter. Check inside your Canadian passport and you'll find a brief message from the foreign affairs minister to the governments of the countries you may find yourself travelling to. There really isn't much to it: "The Minister of Foreign Affairs of Canada requests, in the name of Her Majesty the Queen, all those whom it may concern to allow the bearer to pass freely without let or hindrance and to afford the bearer such assistance and protection as may be necessary." There are two operative phrases there. The first: that this is simply a "request"; we hope other governments honour it, but they're under no obligation to. This is a courtesy far more than it is a right. The other operative phrase is the last part – that the visited country in question help the traveller "as may be necessary." You can be sure that when you murder someone in another country, the government isn't likely to think it necessary to help you out of your jam.

The Canadian passport, valuable as it may be, is not a guarantee that your Charter rights travel with you wherever you go: you certainly couldn't expect to fly to Iran to organize a rally for democracy or women's rights just because you happen to be Canadian. Check the Department of Foreign Affairs' guide for travelling abroad, and it's impossible to miss that conclusion: "You are subject to the criminal justice system of the country where you are imprisoned. Canadian consular officials can provide assistance and support to Canadians in jail. However, they cannot: arrange for your release from prison; post bail, pay lawyers' fees, or pay fines; seek preferential treatment for you; or have you exempted from the due process of local law." When in Rome, you had better behave like a law-abiding Roman or you might well find yourself in an Italian jail, with the Canadian government's blessing.

And what about the responsibilities of being a Canadian citizen? Is citizenship really just a one-way street where living in Canada entitles you to all these rights, without asking anything in return? Obviously that would be absurd. John F. Kennedy clarified the obligations of U.S. citizenship in his 1961 inaugural address, insisting that "defending freedom" was the "responsibility" of all Americans. "Ask not what your country can do for you; ask what you can do for your country," he famously said. Or as Theodore Roosevelt put it, less loftily: "The first requisite of a good citizen in this republic of ours is that he shall be able and willing to pull his own weight."

When people immigrate to Canada, it's not for nothing that the citizenship guide they're required to study in order to become nationals is entitled *Discover Canada: The Rights and Responsibilities of Citizenship.*[10] It's a two-sided coin, a covenant. At the very least, the most basic responsibility requires loyalty to the nation – something the Khadrs, dedicated to fighting our soldiers abroad and killing our innocent citizens, plainly had none of – but there is more to it than that. When new Canadians pledge the Oath of Citizenship, they swear to be "faithful" to the monarch and to "faithfully observe the laws of Canada" – something the murderous Khadrs, again, never saw fit to do. Finally, new citizens swear they will "fulfill my duties as a Canadian citizen." Those duties, clearly, are as much a part of being a citizen of this great country as the rights. The citizenship guide provides a pretty useful framework: obeying the law, obviously, is a big one (though, again, evidently too big for the Khadrs), taking responsibility for providing for yourself and your family, serving on a jury, voting in elections, helping your community, and protecting our heritage and our environment. Even defending Canada, should she require it. These are all things we so often take for granted while still invoking our rights, and yet they form the basic compact we have with our country: none of us can reasonably expect our right to justice to stand if we're not prepared to serve on juries ourselves, or our democratic rights to endure if we refuse to participate in democracy.

The concept of responsibility-free citizenship, promoted, regrettably, by lawyers and the Canadian Bar Association, was most in national vogue during the heyday of Charter excesses, from the mid-1980s to the early 1990s. That was when activist courts, facing an onslaught of challenges from lawyers enthusiastically seizing on the lawsuit opportunities created by the newly entrenched constitution, were busily and radically expanding the definition of Charter rights. That was the era of the Singh decision – the 1985 Supreme Court case that awarded anyone coming to Canada and claiming refugee status the same rights as citizens under the Charter: people who had sworn no duty to Canada were immediately blessed with all its benefits, no matter how legitimate their claim to be here. It was this idea of meaningless citizenship – the insidious, Trudeaupian conceit that one could be a "citizen of the world" (the very title of John English's biography of Trudeau) – that has only gradually begun to be clawed back in recent years by the Conservative government and a more moderate Supreme Court. As Tom Kent, once the principal assistant to former prime minister Lester Pearson, Trudeau's predecessor, said in the wake of the Lebanese evacuation: "Present law permits, even encourages, confusion of loyalties and plurality of citizenship. The sense of a Canadian identity is increasingly diluted."[11]

The Khadrs were beginning to set up their criminal terrorist enterprise in Canada just as that era was dawning. They are an extreme example, but an example nonetheless, of what a country can produce when it so fundamentally mutilates its concept of citizenship to the point that this citizenship implies nearly limitless rights but a complete absence of duty. Ours wasn't the only country to realize, rather belatedly, that it had allowed its notion of citizenship to be so gruesomely bastardized: after 9/11, Australia, France, and the Netherlands, waking up, finally, to the stewing fifth column of Islamists that had taken root inside their borders, quickly began repairing their immigration and citizenship rules, requiring newcomers to accept Western liberal values while demanding they leave their Old World tribal hatreds at home. Canada's latest citizenship guide, a product of Stephen Harper's Conservative government, was part of our own efforts to do the same. "It also asks newcomers to leave their old prejudices and unsavoury rituals at home. No spousal abuse, honour killings or female genital mutilation, please. We're Canadian," cheered Andrew Cohen, then president of the Historica-Dominion Institute. "By contrast . . . in the old guide, the reader was learning about the virtues of recycling, composting, car pooling and conserving energy."[12] Not surprisingly, a lonely Canadian stood up to object: Justin Trudeau, son of the "citizen of the world" and now a Quebec Liberal MP, complained that calling honour killings "barbaric" – as Canada's citizenship guide now does, also applying the term to spousal abuse, female genital mutilation, forced marriage, or other gender-based violence – was an abdication of "responsible neutrality."[13] It is the Trudeau legacy of "neutrality" – the idea that no one value is more worthy than any other and that citizenship is unattached to

Canadian values and responsibilities – that had families like the Khadrs making their homes here.

For all the crying about the Khadr family's "rights" as Canadian citizens, and their naked, greedy exploitation of government-granted privileges, it's an inescapable fact that they failed at every turn to honour their side of the bargain – to uphold the duties that both Ahmed and Maha (since both arrived here when they were older than fourteen) would have had to have sworn to uphold when they took their citizenship oaths. Both egregiously violated those oaths; both of them accepted citizenship here, and the rights that accompany it, under false pretences, by lying about their commitment to our values and their willingness to accept a citizen's duties. Their son Omar has proved he's no better. He's spent his years in Guantanamo hollering about his "rights" as a Canadian, but not once has he (or his legal team, for that matter) articulated how he has maintained his duty to this nation. He betrayed his loyalty to the Queen and to this country; he made himself an enemy of our people, our state, and our allies; and, more elementally, he broke our laws. He murdered an American soldier, for one. He also committed treason. The U.S. government has not charged him with that because he doesn't claim to be an American citizen. But he does claim, still, to be a Canadian one. When he returns, there is nothing to stop our government from charging him as a traitor. He is. And we should.

CHAPTER 7

OMAR KHADR'S CUBAN VACATION

"Khadr was ultimately air evacuated to Bagram Air Base where he was treated in a military field hospital. At Bagram, Khadr underwent surgery for his wounds. Also, the only ophthalmologist in theatre was flown to Afghanistan in order to perform vision-saving eye surgery. The surgery was successful and Khadr's eyesight was saved. Khadr was in the Bagram hospital for two weeks prior to being transferred into the detention facility. Khadr received excellent medical care throughout his time in U.S. custody."

Confession of Omar Ahmed Khadr, October 13, 2010

ood luck calculating all the money the Khadr family has been able to squeeze out of Canadian taxpayers whenever it was convenient to cash in on their citizenship and run back to the indulgent arms of this country whenever they needed it. No matter that this was a country they were at war with overseas. There was not one but two open-heart surgeries at Toronto's Sick Kids hospital to repair the congenital defect of infant Ibrahim Khadr. And the operations at one of Canada's top trauma centres, Sunnybrook Health Sciences Centre, to save the arm of Ahmed Khadr after his brush with explosives in Afghanistan. And the ongoing medical care and support of Kareem Khadr, now living in Canada, paralyzed from the waist down after a firefight against Pakistani troops, the one that killed his dad. (He's all right with it: "I'm still pretty happy that I didn't get paralyzed from a car accident or a gang shooting or something," he told *Maclean's* magazine a few years back.[1] "You know, at least I was there helping my father. I had a cause to be there.")

These are handouts well into the six figures for a family that detested Canada and avoided it as much as possible, preferring to dwell among, and fight crusaders alongside, their fellow jihadis abroad. In all those years plotting against the West from inside Osama bin Laden's compound, how much federal income tax do you suppose the Khadrs remitted to the Canadian government in return? Who knows even how to calculate the value of having a sitting Canadian prime minister use his precious time on an Asian trade mission to personally lobby the prime minister of Pakistan to go easy on a terrorist in the custody of her security staff.

But compared to the bills the beleaguered taxpayer of the United States of America would have to foot for Omar Khadr, Canadians should be grateful they've got off relatively easy.

It is an irony not recognized nearly often enough that had Omar Khadr somehow been free to pursue the lifestyle he aspired toward, he would almost certainly be living in far greater misery than anything he's experienced at the U.S. naval prison at Guantanamo Bay. The average American prisoner, with his three square meals daily, the roof over his head, his supply of fresh water and free access to dentists and doctors, already enjoys a lifestyle miles better than that of the majority of people unlucky enough to have been born in Third World countries like Afghanistan and Pakistan. But even the residents of Sing Sing and Leavenworth penitentiaries must be green with envy at the comparatively comfortable lifestyle America's worst enemies, the inmates of Gitmo, get to enjoy courtesy of three hundred million Americans, all of whom these prisoners would murder in a heartbeat in the name of Allah.

Guantanamo isn't the Four Seasons, of course. It's not even Club Med. But there's a reason that inmates there pack on an average of twenty pounds not long after they arrive, and it isn't just because of ice-cream Mondays. Or ice-cream Fridays (they have both).[2] Or all the free Pepsi they enjoy. Though that's all part of it.

More to the point, it's because life as a dutiful al Qaeda soldier is likely "hell," as an attorney for Human Rights Watch in Afghanistan has explained.[3] "Those guys showed up [at Guantanamo] half-starved, some of them probably hadn't had a proper hot meal since the war began. It wouldn't be hard to put on weight."

When North Americans imagine the conditions that inmates at Guantanamo might be living in, we can't help but compare them to the quality of life that we're used to in our comfy homes. But the Taliban and al Qaeda fighters living in Guantanamo didn't have a previous address in a Toronto suburb or a Vancouver condominium. They lived in Afghanistan and Waziristan, the tribal terror haven along the Pakistani border. At home, their existence was "peasant life" – in mud huts, with little to no modern health care, plagued by poverty and constant violence, scarcely a school or hospital for miles.[4] By UNICEF's statistics, Afghanistan is the second-worst country on the planet for kids dying – 20 per cent of little kids perish before their fifth birthday; more than 13 per cent of kids before their first birthday – while the average family survives on roughly one dollar a day. Just 48 per cent of Afghanis have access to "improved drinking water sources" – in rural areas, just 39 per cent do – while just 37 per cent of the entire population of Afghanistan has access to modern sanitation facilities. The average life expectancy in Afghanistan is only forty-four years.[5]

On the road, hunting infidels, life is even more short, nasty, and brutish, as fighters scurry between dusty hidey-holes, subsisting on a few handfuls of food while dodging bullets and bombs, sleeping in the elements in freezing weather and sweltering summers.[6] Meanwhile, boys as young as thirteen and up to their late teens who join the fight – youngsters like Omar Khadr – serve double duty: when they're not shooting infidels as soldiers, they're exploited as the sexual playthings – the "dancing boys" – of their abusive Taliban masters.[7]

This is important to remember not because the United States should be doing the terrorists at Guantanamo Bay, like Khadr, any big favours. It's not that the U.S. owes them the better shelter, food, water, personal safety, and health care they're getting – miles better than anything they'd likely ever experience in their entire lives in Afghanistan. After all, the Americans are still denying them the one great pleasure in their lives: killing infidels. But it's necessary to keep in mind when terrorist sympathizers, like those in Omar Khadr's fan club, whine about the terrible conditions that Guantanamo inmates live in. In fact, Kyndra Rotunda, a former army prosecutor at Guantanamo, revealed in 2011 that a number of prisoners at Guantanamo had "asked to stay in Gitmo" even after being offered release. "They prefer captivity in Gitmo to freedom in their own countries," which was so much worse than the comfortable lives they had found in the navy prison, she said.[8] Before Omar Khadr was caught that day attacking American troops, he had already chosen voluntarily to live in terrible conditions – a lifestyle less comfortable, less secure, less healthy, and in many ways worse than anything he'd experience in U.S. custody.

That much was clear from the very start with the first thing American troops did to Omar Khadr. These were the men he had been attacking mercilessly, refusing to surrender even after being given multiple opportunities, continuing to fight till his gang had seriously wounded Layne Morris and he had mortally wounded Christopher Speer. And when they found him there, half dead, bleeding, ripped open, what was their first action?

To save his life.

While Khadr cursed the soldiers with his fading breaths and demanded they make a martyr of him so he could collect his promised reward in the afterlife for dying while murdering a Christian, they acted, instead, only and utterly humanely. At the time, they had no way of knowing that Khadr was a high-value capture, a young man who inherited the networks of his crime family, networks extending all the way to al Qaeda's most senior figures. They wouldn't have known he was a Canadian citizen. This teenager lying in the middle of an Afghan wasteland certainly wouldn't have looked the part. Complying with his request – to shoot him right there and then, moments after he had blown up Christopher Speer, after he had fought these soldiers so relentlessly in a firefight lasting hours – could have been a very powerful temptation. It must have seemed impossible that anyone would even care. Even just to let him die, to suffocate on his own blood, right there in the Afghan mud, would have been a simple thing to do. It might not even have taken very long for him to succumb to his serious injuries, including two bullets in his thorax.

Instead, U.S. medics rushed to save Omar Khadr's life, providing him critical medical care right there in the field. "We had two medics that day and he killed the first one," Special Forces Sgt. Layne Morris, who lost his eye when Khadr's al Qaeda cell attacked him and his fellow troops, told Global News in 2005. "The second one saved his life. He would have bled to death from his injuries in a short amount of time."[9]

The American military medevaced him to Bagram Air Base, where American doctors sewed him back together. And those doctors arranged to fly an ophthalmologist to Afghanistan all the way from Kuwait to operate on Khadr's left eye, which had been damaged by shrapnel. Even if the U.S. military had begun by then to realize that Khadr might have some valuable intelligence, it's virtually impossible to imagine how he'd be any less useful with just one eye. And yet, the Americans flew in a top U.S. ophthalmologist to successfully operate on and save Khadr's eye just the same.[10]

Omar Khadr's first experience as a captive of the American military was a free operation from a U.S. eye surgeon, in a country where the average citizen could not hope for such lavish medical care – or, really, even far more basic health care – for no other reason than that it seemed the humane thing to do.

But while the United States would imprison and aggressively prosecute Khadr, this life-saving and vision-saving medical care wasn't the last time he would benefit from America's mercy. Khadr, of course, spent his early years at Guantanamo Bay alleging he was being "tortured" – something all al Qaeda operatives are trained to do. A raid on an al Qaeda cell in England turned up the terrorist group's manual on war tactics; if captured, the manual advises its members "the brothers must insist on proving that torture was inflicted on them by state security before the judge. Complain of mistreatment while in prison."[11]

Claims about alleged brutalities against inmates at Gitmo – including a *Newsweek* report that guards had flushed a Koran down a toilet – have been proven to be fraudulent.[12] When lawyers at Omar Khadr's murder trial presented a tape of what some of this alleged "torture" looked like when he arrived at the prison, the video showed American guards struggling to get Khadr to cooperate and step on a scale to be weighed, something Red Cross directives require. He tried to resist, wriggling and fighting, claiming he had to go to the bathroom, and then crying.[13] All because he didn't want to be weighed. "Am I an animal?" Khadr demanded to know, before composing himself enough to promise the guards, "Sooner or later, God will take our revenge and he's going to send on you people who will torture you."

Suffice it to say that plenty of U.S. prisoners would be just fine with some of the "torture" that Guantanamo Bay inmates have been forced to suffer. The interrogation rooms, as one expert in criminal psychiatry remarked, "are far more comfortable than interview rooms found in American jails, and resemble day rooms/visitor rooms in many hospitals."[14]

Prisoners at Guantanamo have their meals catered by the same company that supplies food to college students in such American schools as the University of Michigan – except everything sent to Gitmo is certified Halal.[15] They get three hot meals a day (even the high-security-risk detainees, kept in isolation, get two meals served piping hot to their cells, and a cold lunch). Medical inspectors actually routinely test the food "for proper temperature, quality, hygiene, and freshness," reports Gordon Cullucu, an author and former soldier who personally investigated living conditions at Gitmo after hearing so many disturbing reports in the media about the conditions there.[16] "Food temperature at the serving point has to be within a seven-degree window," he notes. If any meal fails to meet those standards, "it gets tossed on the spot."

Research by a *Slate* magazine reporter found that the prisoners' menu revolved around "Asian-accented stews of beef, chicken and fish"; "a host of legumes: black beans, lentils, kidney beans and chickpeas"; rice, bagels, "pita bread, baguettes [and] sliced wheat bread" – all of which are fresh baked on site.[17] If prisoners behave, they get "cakes and dates and other treats." Those dates, as it happens, aren't the sort you'll find in your average North American supermarket: they're bigger, and juicier, and ordered specially for the Guantanamo terrorists. They cost a fortune.[18]

Inmates with big appetites are also "provided 'additional servings' if they request them."[19] During Ramadan, the administrators at Guantanamo ensured that any prisoners observing the daylight fast got an "early, pre-dawn breakfast" and a "late, post-sunset dinner" so they could adhere to their customs while still eating well. At the end of the holiday, Muslims traditionally have a big feast to celebrate, something guards "worked hard to prepare a special meal" for.[20] For this feast of Eid, Cullucu noted that the menu included "parsley salad, chicken kabsa, Saudi rice, grilled shish kebab, dates, honey, yogurt, fruit, orange juice, and milk." Meanwhile, any prisoners with special dietary requirements – if they're lactose intolerant, have allergies, or maybe have developed diabetes from eating too much Guantanamo ice cream, Pepsi, and cake – get specially made, individualized meals.[21] Actually, even if an inmate decides he doesn't care for a certain kind of food or ingredient – say, carrots – "food service specialists must make certain that no carrot-containing items are included," Cullucu reports. "No steamed carrots, no peas and carrots, no carrot cake, no carrots in his salad . . ." Some detainees can request that certain food items not be served touching other food items.

"Regardless of the inanity of the request," Cullucu discovered, "Guantánamo supervisory officials honor it." No wonder it costs American taxpayers twice as much to keep a Gitmo detainee fed – about $34 a day – than it does to feed a U.S. soldier in Iraq or Afghanistan. All in all, at Guantanamo Bay, the number of daily calories served up to detainees goes up to 4,200.[22] By comparison, in Afghanistan, the average person's caloric intake is about 1,900 calories – just about 72 per cent of the minimum their body needs.[23]

Even Omar Khadr was impressed with the service. In a letter to his mom a month after arriving at Guantanamo, he wrote, "The Americans are the opposite of what the whole world [says]. Health services 24 hours, three meals a day, Ramadan eat before dawn and sunset."[24]

With all that Halal, specialty food being offered up to al Qaeda terrorists three times a day, with every special food request catered to, and the most careful attention to health and hygiene, Guantanamo might look to the average U.S. prison inmate more like a Disney cruise for extra-picky eaters than a prison, let alone the "gulag of our time," as Amnesty International's general secretary hyperbolically described it in 2005.[25] This, to refer to a place where residents get their very own tutors, homeschooling them in "astronomy, math, grammar, Shakespeare, even elocution."[26] Such hardship. Did the Soviets pipe satellite TV into their gulag's "communal living" spaces, like they do at Gitmo? Or offer "movie night" once a week? Did inmates get access to refrigerators, stoves, microwaves, washers, and dryers? What about ping-pong tables, exercise machines, couches, or a library stuffed with more than five thousand books?[27, 28] Did Soviet exiles get fans to keep them cool on a rare, warm Siberian summer day?[29] Would Stalin have ensured that every Muslim detainee had his very own copy of the Koran – available in any number of different languages – and helpful arrows showing him the direction to pray toward Mecca, as well as prayer rugs and beads and oils, and a helpful call to prayer, five times a day, in seventeen different languages?[30] Do you think he'd build basketball courts for his captives?[31] Guantanamo inmates get to spend up to eight hours a day in the recreation yard, playing sports, praying with one another, or just socializing, with ready access to Gatorade to quench their deep-down body thirst.[32] These are all amenities provided to inmates at Guantanamo Bay. Were Stalin alive today, you can be sure he would have a good hearty laugh at the United States for letting their worst, most avowed enemies, men like Omar Khadr – not imprisoned for dissent, like inmates in the gulag, but with the actual blood of America's soldiers on their hands – spend the day playing video games on a Nintendo Wii and PlayStation.[33]

All these things, mind you, were the creature comforts afforded to the average Yusuf al-Shmoe detained at the U.S. navy's Cuban resort. But for the favoured son of Canada's first family of terror, even all of this wasn't enough. Omar Khadr wanted more. And, astonishingly, he usually got what he wanted.

Canada's Consular Affairs and Justice officials certainly did their best to accommodate whatever wishes Omar had. They even made sure he was flush with goodies he didn't ask for. On one March 2008 visit, one bureaucrat reported that she came bearing "candy, fresh fruit, nuts, some junk food" and "fresh squeezed orange juice" as well as "warmed up lasagna."[34] While on the subject of food, Omar began rattling off a list of demands to suit his other culinary preferences. "He asked that we request he be given a side of cheese and olives every meal," the official reported. He had "previously asked for a side of olive oil with lunch," a bottle of which had been readily purchased and delivered to him by another bureaucrat. And apparently, the guards had been advised that this would be a requirement for the finicky diner from now on because, when they delivered lunch, the government worker noted, they brought him a "hamburger with lettuce and tomato, a small side salad of lettuce, a side of olive oil and a container of apple juice." Since he was full of lasagna, he pushed aside the burger, even though, the official noted, "hamburgers and the fettuccine alfredo . . . were among the only meals he liked." In fact, he even had consular officials talk to the guards about preparing more Italian dishes "for which Omar had expressed a preference."[35] Omar was apparently one very demanding customer.

Canadian government officials sure spent a lot of time procuring him all kinds of food, clothing, and entertainment items. He asked them for new shoes, ones that were better for his new hobby of running – they should be Skechers, Omar specified, because he "really liked" that brand; they brought him a new pillow; he asked them to bring him a pair of sunglasses because the light at Guantanamo bothered his eyes. They brought him books and magazines. And more. Here is just a partial – repeat: *partial* – list of the things Omar Khadr sent government officials to procure for him: [36, 37]

> A photo book of Canada; chocolates; chips; green and black tea; coffee; chewing gum; shampoo and conditioner; body wash; a running logbook; a "variety of *National Geographic, Modern Science* and *Nature* magazines" as well as magazines about cars; novels and non-fiction books; dominoes; a medical textbook; strawberries; Tin Tin comics; salad dressing; pistachios; an origami book with paper; a yoga book; special seeds available only at "Middle Eastern grocery stores"; moisturizer; and cologne.

Believe it or not, these generous Canadian government officials did their best to get him all of these. If Omar Khadr's supporters here in Canada wondered why the federal government wasn't doing more to help their man out of his legal bind in Gitmo, it may just be because officials were too busy running around like his personal assistants on shopping trips. In all, Canadian taxpayers spent thousands of dollars catering to the whims of an al Qaeda soldier. [38]

Khadr wasn't just waited on, literally hand and foot, by the Canadian government.

After getting patched up by top U.S. doctors, Khadr continued to avail himself of the kind of gold-standard medical care his fellow assassins in Afghanistan could only dream about. He had three separate medical visits just for his dandruff. He had his ears flushed, a wart removed, and he got creams for acne and dry skin complaints.[39] After Khadr chipped a tooth, the navy sent him a dentist to fix it right up.[40] (The base has full dental care facilities that offer everything from routine dental work to oral surgery to implants and dentures.[41]) He was seen regularly by a gastroenterologist, who prescribed him pills for his upset stomach: no waiting in medicare queues like the average Canadian has to do to see a specialist.[42] In fact, prisoners older than fifty at Guantanamo are offered free colonoscopies, to watch for cancer,[43] and unlike many Canadian hospitals, Gitmo has on-site an MRI, CAT scan, ultrasound machines, and "ultramodern digitalized X-ray equipment in their hospital that is not available to the soldiers and civilians at the Guantánamo Base."[44] When Khadr complained of leg discomfort, he was sent right over to the medical staff, who promptly X-rayed his knees. They didn't find any problems, but, to keep their inmate happy, they offered him arthroscopic surgery and physiotherapy.[45] He was given repeated CT scans and MRI studies, "workups for various auto-immune diseases," and eye appointments every three to four months. For complaints about foot pain, he received special "comfort socks" and cushioned shoe insoles.[46]

The camp even offers psychologists to residents needing therapy. It's little wonder that Canadian officials would learn from talking to Guantanamo staff that the medical care inmates receive is "superior to what many American citizens have access to."[47] When a Pakistani prisoner was scheduled for heart bypass surgery, a full surgical team was flown down from Bethesda, Maryland, on a special aircraft, with all the necessary crew and equipment. The cost of the arrangements was estimated at roughly half a million dollars.[48] Once the entire surgery was ready to go, the patient abruptly changed his mind. He was, guards figured, "just jerking us around"; they called it a "victory for al Qaeda."

When Omar wasn't busy running or playing basketball – he told Canadian officials he had access to "almost all the exercise I want"[49] – watching movies, or reading the magazines, comic books, and novels arriving in his lavish care packages, he was offered access to a pretty decent education at Guantanamo too – this time in something other than the Jew-hating and bomb-making that his parents taught him. He took classes in French, Arabic, Pashto, and English.[50] Canadian officials brought him math and French textbooks and workbooks and negotiated with the American government to fund interactive "distance learning" through an Ottawa school, even if Khadr seemed to prefer spending time with his comics and car magazines instead.[51]

Your average overprivileged North American teenager might occasionally whine about the drudgery of school and call it "torture." Omar Khadr, who repeatedly hollered "torture" – as any well-prepared al Qaeda soldier knows to do – may have actually meant it. Sure, by commonly accepted, Western liberal definitions of torture, as broad as they are, Khadr never faced anything more violent than when a pair of U.S. soldiers tried nudging him onto a scale so he could be weighed according to Red Cross conventions. When lawyers produced the actual videotape of that weigh-in, it was suddenly obvious to anyone who saw it how flagrant were Omar Khadr's lies about abuse. It shouldn't have been a surprise: a man who was eager to kill Americans surely wouldn't hesitate to deceive them.

And so Khadr made up stories claiming he'd been tortured from his time at the hospital at Bagram Air Base, where he was actually having his life saved by American medical staff, all the way to his cushy stay at Guantanamo. In reality, his own mother told reporters in 2005 that she was hearing regularly from her son. "He's fine," she said.[52] She was assured by the International Committee of the Red Cross that her son was in the "best of conditions," she wrote in 2003,[53] and in a letter to Omar the following year, she wrote, "I know your mental health is excellent, that your self-esteem is sky-high."[54]

In August 2010, when Khadr's dubious claims about abuse were finally tested impartially in a court of law rather than being swallowed whole by his sycophants in the Canadian media, the judge overseeing Khadr's war crimes trial determined that there was "no credible evidence the accused was ever tortured . . . even using a liberal interpretation considering the accused's age."[55]

But then, for Omar Khadr, being stuck at Guantanamo instead of blowing up Canadian and American soldiers with those landmines he had become so proficient at building must have felt like sadism. Spending his days eating three specially prepared hot meals, playing video games, and watching World Cup soccer and movies on his satellite TV instead of wiring up instruments of murder with a gang of unwashed, toothless fanatics in some mud-walled cellar must have been utter agony. And surely, learning all that math and French could only have felt like torture to someone used to learning only fun things, like how evil Jews and Christians are and the best ways of killing them en masse. Khadr had never really spent much time in school before.[56] You don't need to know dull things like algebra, or how to conjugate verbs, if you're going to spend your short life building improvised explosive devices before you're turned into a martyr by U.S. artillery. Thriving, well fed, healthy, and comfortable amid all the amenities of Guantanamo Bay was certainly not the life Omar Khadr wanted; it wasn't like the Islamist utopia he was fighting to restore. After all, at least under the enlightened Taliban, only about one in six school-aged children had to suffer through an education,[57] and likely none of them had to endure any lessons as rigorous and useful as those of a North American curriculum.

But then, they don't get to spend their days playing video games, practising yoga, and enjoying free ice cream, Pepsi, and cheeseburgers either.

CHAPTER 8

THE OMAR KHADR FAN CLUB

"Khadr considered himself to be an active member of al Qaeda and he shared the same goals as the organization, which are to target and kill all Americans, whether civilian or military, anywhere they can be found and to 'plunder their money.'"

Confession of Omar Ahmed Khadr, October 13, 2010

Maybe Canada should be ashamed about our history with Omar Khadr. Perhaps we should be embarrassed that we allowed his family to use our country as a safe haven to which they could flee whenever they needed free health care or to raise money for their criminal activities. Or rueful that our gullible prime minister brought the power of his office to bear on the Pakistani government to let the Khadrs off the hook for a terrorist attack in which the patriarch of the gang was, as it turns out, pretty clearly guilty. Or that our government allowed the family to funnel money to terrorists overseas. But that's not why Omar Khadr's biggest supporters think we should be ashamed. Khadr's biggest fans think we should be ashamed because, well, we "abandoned" him.[1] Because we are a "heathen" country where citizens are viciously driven by "prejudices" against Muslims.[2] Because we support the "farce" of the U.S. military hearings.[3]

Of course you'd expect Khadr's family or his al Qaeda compatriots to think the worst of us for supporting the infidel Americans' right to try a terrorist who attacked and killed one of its citizens. But those quotes, those scoldings of Canada, didn't come from Khadr's fellow jihadis. They didn't even come from the reprehensible Zaynab Khadr, Omar's sister and courier for al Qaeda, or Omar's mother, Maha Khadr, hater of all things Canadian and Osama bin Laden's most passionate cheerleader. They came from Omar Khadr's vociferous fan club, his most passionate admirers of all.

They came from the Canadian media.

Omar Khadr may be what most people recognize as a "fifth column" in Western society: enemy supporters who lurk among us seeking to destroy us from within. But once he was gone, locked away safely in a U.S. jail cell, citizens here would discover an entirely different breed of collaborator: the Canadian journalism profession.

"Shame on us," railed *The Globe and Mail's* top political columnist, Lawrence Martin. We should forget considering ourselves a "progressive, fair-minded people who believe in equal rights before the law," he wrote in 2010. By supporting the U.S. trial of Khadr, we are clearly just a "heathen" country driven by "primal prejudices."[4] Got that? In the matter of a murderous Islamist terrorist driven by hatred to kill Jews and Christians who, in fact, derived pleasure from it,[5] average Canadians are the bigoted heathens, according to one of the biggest columnists at one of the biggest newspapers in the country.

The Globe and Mail actually considers itself the country's newspaper of record, and in this case, it would appear that the assessment that *The Globe* stands as the nation's official representative of the general tenor and attitude of journalists across the country isn't that far off. When it comes to Canadian self-loathing and sympathy for Canada's own, homegrown al Qaeda devil, Lawrence Martin, after all, is hardly alone.

"Shame on Canada for failing to object" to the Americans' "kangaroo court," wrote the *Toronto Star*'s veteran national affairs columnist, Thomas Walkom, in 2009.[6] The United States was conducting nothing better than a "low level show trial," he said, as if he were nonchalantly equating one of the world's oldest, most robust democracies and leading champion of human rights and rule of law to justice-mocking regimes like Iran, North Korea, and China. Perhaps it's not surprising that Walkom should be so outraged that the United States would have the temerity to try Khadr in a military court as a prisoner of war: a year before he dismissed the Americans as enemies of justice, he determined that Omar Khadr wasn't nearly as bad as the United States – and the Canadian government, for that matter – would have us believe. No, he decided, Omar Khadr was a victim of circumstance vilified by a pair of North American regimes run amok. So what if he was discovered holed up in an al Qaeda compound? So what if he was captured after a brutal firefight that claimed the lives of a U.S. medic? "It now seems he may have been just a kid who for whatever reason . . . ended up getting shot in the back," Walkom concluded.[7]

That perspective seems to have infected newsrooms across the country. In Quebec, columnist Ivy Weir, working for *The Record* in Sherbrooke, decided that Omar Khadr may well exhibit all the qualities of a "young hero."[8]

Much like the insouciant Zaynab Khadr – who called Chris Speer's death "no big deal" – she wasn't terribly moved by the fact that Khadr had attacked and murdered a U.S. military medic and father of two. "People at war get killed," Weir shrugged. In fact, she figured, "Omar Khadr is being condemned for the very qualities we would have admired had they been exercised on our behalf": he stood bravely for his cause against the onslaught of U.S. bullets and bombs (she didn't mention that the Americans had given Khadr repeated opportunities to surrender) and he remained loyal to his father's ideals and convictions (which happened to include the conviction to murder innocent people). "Had such acts been perpetrated on our own side of this war, we would have pinned medals on him." Of course anyone could apply the same facile logic to Nazis in the Second World War. You won't find many Canadian journalists with enough chutzpah to complain that those stouthearted members of the ss were being unfairly "vilified" where they might, with a different per-spective, be "admired," as Weir argued about Omar Khadr.

And Naomi Lakritz, a columnist for the *Calgary Herald*, the biggest paper in Canada's fifth-biggest news-paper market, eagerly nodded along with the idea that the Americans had no better claim to ideals of justice than some of the world's most dishonourable regimes. Khadr, she wrote, "doesn't stand a chance of getting a fair trial" from the U.S. military.[9] "The Bulgarian and Mexican justice systems are seen as corrupt and undemocratic, but Guantanamo should be viewed in the same light." The fact that there was so much evidence of "tortures taking place at Guantanamo" was proof that Khadr's trial would prove a mockery of justice.

Of course, we now have the facts about so-called torture at Guantanamo. We know that the White House authorized waterboarding on three senior al Qaeda bosses: Khalid Sheikh Mohammed, Abu Zubaydah, and Abd al-Rahim al-Nashiri. Mohammed was the architect of mass murder behind 9/11, by the way; Zubaydah was the go-to man between Osama bin Laden and the global network of al Qaeda cells and seems to have procured the funds to finance the 9/11 attacks; and al-Nashiri confessed to being a key coordinator in the 2000 bombing of the USS *Cole*, which killed seventeen Americans.[10] Now, whether waterboarding is torture or not is a matter of much debate, but no matter who's right, we know this much: it was used on only those three arch terrorists (and, as revealed in Justice Department memos, the intensive interrogation technique resulted in Mohammed giving up valuable information that allowed the CIA to intercept and thwart al Qaeda's plans for a massive, 9/11–style "second wave" terrorist attack against Los Angeles[11]). We also know that tens of thousands of Americans have been waterboarded too – the U.S. military uses it to prepare soldiers for interrogation should they ever be captured.[12] And we know something else: it was never used on Omar Khadr.

We also know that most other allegations of so-called abuses or torture lack any real evidence to back them up. We already know that al Qaeda operatives are trained specifically to cry "torture," knowing it will undermine the reputation and determination of their captors in countries like the United States. Al Qaeda training manuals instruct that "brothers must insist on proving that torture was inflicted on them by state security before the judge. Complain of mistreatment while in prison."[13] It's a clever and perfect tactic of asymmetrical warfare: exploit the human rights conscience of liberal democracies by putting out messages of torture through credulous news media, making conscientious citizens of countries like the United States and Canada squirm uncomfortably. Scores of Guantanamo inmates have done just that, and yet, a Pentagon review into allegations of abuse by the navy inspector general found that, in twenty-four thousand interrogations, there were just three substantiated "minor" cases of abuse.[14] These consisted of one assault and two instances of female guards making sexually suggestive gestures to detainees. Again, you'd have to define the term *torture* pretty broadly to capture that kind of behaviour, but even if you wanted to consider a woman squeezing her breasts together abuse – and for fundamentalist Muslim jihadi fanatics, a woman merely daring to act as an equal, with her face uncovered, let alone as a superior, asking questions of him, must be both humiliating and offensive – none of those minor incidents involved Omar Khadr.

The "interrogation memos" the Obama administration released in 2009, meanwhile, uncovered hardly anything that would qualify as any more horrific. They revealed specifics about the "enhanced interrogation" techniques approved by the Bush administration at Guantanamo. These included: grasping a detainee's shirt; pushing him against a "flexible false wall," while his "head and neck are supported with a rolled hood or towel that provides a c-collar effect to help prevent whiplash"; the interrogator putting his palms on the cheeks of the detainee; slapping the detainee's face, "not to inflict physical pain . . . [but] to induce shock, surprise, and/or humiliation"; placing a prisoner in a confined space where he "can stand up or sit down" for a maximum of eighteen hours, or one where he can only sit, for a maximum of two hours; having a detainee lean against a wall, putting his body weight against his fingertips, kneeling and leaning backward, or sitting on the floor with hands above his head, to "induce muscle fatigue"; and sleep deprivation.[15] One special technique designed just for Zubaydah was to place him in a confined space with "a harmless insect such as a caterpillar" because he was afraid of insects.

It goes without saying that none of this compares to the shocking torture and brutalities routinely practised in the countries where these Guantanamo inmates come from. As the future (and now former) Liberal leader Michael Ignatieff pointed out when he was still a human rights professor at Harvard University, these are, after all, "dangerous" prisoners of war and so, treating them slightly worse than teenaged shoplifters should not be considered "as some example of the basic brutality and immorality of the American empire." In places such as Egypt,[16] Jordan,[17] and Kuwait,[18] arrested terrorists end up beaten with cables, electro-shocked, hung by their wrists or ankles, and raped with broomsticks. But even if we insist upon holding the United States to a higher standard of treatment for its war captives than they'd get back in their home countries – and we absolutely should insist on it – and even if we broaden our definition of "abuse" to include shirt-grasping, muscle-fatigue, and caterpillar exposure, the fact remains: none of these techniques, not a single one, was ever used on Omar Khadr.

In fact, there was never any solid evidence anywhere to suggest that Omar Khadr – despite his uncorroborated and, ultimately, debunked claims that while at Guantanamo he was suffocated until he passed out; that people pulled his hair, spit in his face, and kneed him in the thighs; and that he had to sleep in a cold cell, was dropped on the floor, and rolled around in his own urine after wetting himself – faced anything less than kid glove treatment. There is, however, a preponderance of evidence for anyone willing to look, that Khadr was provided exceptionally gentle treatment from the moment he was captured. At Afghanistan's Bagram Air Base, where he was first treated and questioned before being transferred to Guantanamo, when staff noticed Khadr felt some pain when he had his bandages changed, they pre-medicated him before changing his dressings so he would be more comfortable.[19] As one nurse later reported, adhering to just the minimal requirements that the Geneva Conventions requires for prisoner of war treatment wasn't even sufficient for these medical professionals; they had committed themselves to higher standards, even in cases of soldier-killers like Omar Khadr. "We were guided by principles of best practices of nursing, rather than the Geneva Convention," said Lt. Col. Donna Hershey, the head nurse at the Bagram hospital.[20] When doctors reviewed Khadr's medical records, they found no sign of any injuries that would be consistent with man-handling or violence from interrogators.[21] And when Khadr was allowed to explain in person, rather than through an affidavit carefully written for shock value by his sympathetic and media-savvy lawyers, what kinds of torture he experi-enced, he mentioned being screamed at and being told that he might be sexually assaulted in prison.[22] Outside of that, Khadr suspiciously failed to mention in letters to his family, in visits with his defence team, or to his friends anything about being tortured – and when one psychiatrist directly asked him about it, he seemed bored and uninterested and, according to the doctor, exhibited the "ennui of a person who did not want to be bothered with the details."[23]

That, of course, didn't stop Canadian journalists from regurgitating Khadr's claims of torture as if they were fact and lining up to support their little Guantanamo lamb. Michelle Shephard was the *Toronto Star*'s national secu-rity correspondent and, as a reporter assigned to the Khadr saga, became the lens through which readers of Canada's largest daily newspaper would learn of his unproven alle-gations of torture. She would go on not only to write an entire book about it, called *Guantanamo's Child*, but also to speak in Edmonton following a 2008 student rally organized in support of Omar Khadr.[24] The *Toronto Star* may be notoriously left wing – its immutable liberal philosophy is actually codified in its very constitution[25] – but even its readers seemed to perceive a credulity in Shephard's coverage of the "child" that they couldn't ignore. The reporter has said she's received emails urging her to marry Omar Khadr.[26]

Maybe her readers were being sarcastic – some, she said, had told her she should move to Gitmo too – but then again, maybe not. Shephard filed no fewer than 238 stories to the *Star* since his capture, including numerous stories detailing the pleas and protestations of his lawyers, parents, and grandparents, including all manner of torture claims.[27] In the acknowledgements to her book she actually thanks the reprehensible Maha and Zaynab Khadr, who "took me into their confidence and spent hours explaining Omar's upbringing."[28]

But Shephard's efforts were sparing in comparison to Canada's national television and radio broadcaster: according to its website, the CBC has produced 1,700 stories about Khadr. Compare that to the kind of attention it pays to men of peace like the Dalai Lama, who only gets 1,550 stories, or Nelson Mandela, who's only merited 1,070 stories[29] – despite both having been making news for years before Canadians even heard the name Omar Khadr. Judy Rebick, a former CBC host, wrote on her blog a love letter to Khadr that makes her sound like a preteen swooning over Justin Bieber. "My heart aches for Omar Khadr," she wrote. She compared him to a "super hero" – beaten down by "the system only to emerge so strong and skilful."

She praises his "dignity" and hopes someday he "will emerge from this nightmare as a strong and powerful figure along the lines of Nelson Mandela."[30] She doesn't seem interested in mentioning that he was being held not for protesting an apartheid system that discriminated against him for the colour of his skin, as Mandela was, but because he murdered a young father of two small children who, just days before he died, had walked into an Afghanistan minefield to rescue two wounded Afghan children trapped there.[31] Those kinds of heroics, apparently, don't touch Rebick's heart.

Perhaps Rebick is suffering from a variant of Stockholm syndrome. After all, the woman is an ardent advocate for gay rights, she's Jewish, and is one of Canada's leading feminists (she was once head of the National Action Committee on the Status of Women, at the time Canada's largest women's lib organization). She may have somehow developed a crush on an Islamic fundamentalist, homophobic, misogynist, anti-Semite, but you can be sure the feeling is anything but mutual. Sure, Khadr might have daydreamed about Judy Rebick too, if he knew she existed. But his dreams would have been the pleasant dreams of killing yet another infidel.

CHAPTER 9

OPPOSITION OPPORTUNISM ON OMAR KHADR

"In addition to Omar Khadr and the other al Qaeda cell members, there were both women and children in the compound. Prior to, and throughout the course of the firefight and during breaks in the firing, U.S. forces gave the occupants inside the compound multiple chances to surrender. At one point, the women and children in the compound exited the compound and U.S. forces escorted them to safety. Khadr had the opportunity to leave with the women and children. At that time, he could have left the compound and was not forced by anyone to stay and fight."

Confession of Omar Ahmed Khadr, October 13, 2010

The fact that Omar Khadr's life in Guantanamo Bay was pretty mild, especially given the villainy of his beliefs and the gravity of his crimes, and even more so when contrasted against the kind of fate he might have faced had he not been captured by soldiers of an exceptionally humane country, was not lost on Michael Ignatieff.

In 2002, the future (and now former) leader of Canada's federal Liberal Party was still working at Harvard University as director of the Carr Center for Human Rights Policy, where he was among the most respected and revered thinkers on matters of human rights in the world. And when he was interviewed by *Maclean's* magazine about whether he thought it was advisable for Canadian soldiers in Afghanistan to cooperate in turning over captured Taliban and al Qaeda fighters to U.S. forces if they knew they could end up in Guantanamo, Ignatieff made it clear that he was perfectly aware of how lucky these captives were.[1]

He said he firmly "believed they will be" accorded the protections of the Geneva Convention (he was right; they were) and that they were far better off in American custody than the alternative. "What I would say is missing from that debate is two facts," he told the interviewer. "One is that if these prisoners weren't in Guantanamo, and if they had been in the custody of the Northern Alliance [an anti-Taliban militia] they would probably be dead. Secondly, these are dangerous individuals. I don't regard their treatment as some example of the basic brutality and immorality of the American empire."

Of course, that was back when Michael Ignatieff was a professor: he could be as freethinking and sensible as he wanted to. It was his job, actually. But a few years later, he would leave Harvard, lured north to his birthplace of Canada by Liberal Party heavyweights shopping for new political leadership blood. Somewhere en route to becoming the leader of Canada's Official Opposition Party – a job requiring the routine condemnation of the government and the prime minister, Stephen Harper – Ignatieff suddenly decided he didn't trust those suspect Americans to administrate proper justice to their terrorist detainees after all. Suddenly those captured detainees weren't so "dangerous." Suddenly the American empire was very much showing "brutality" toward these poor, lost Taliban souls. Ignatieff began insisting that the U.S. was violating Omar Khadr's most basic rights,[2] calling the American military tribunals unfair and illegitimate,[3] and demanding that the prison at Guantanamo be permanently shuttered.[4]

Under Ignatieff's leadership, the Liberal Party's official line became that the Harper government had abandoned poor Omar Khadr to the depravity of an inferior, untrustworthy jailer in the form of the American government.

To be fair, Ignatieff wasn't the only Liberal to suddenly flip flop and start spinning Omar Khadr's U.S. custody into some kind of gross and intolerable injustice. His whole party, remember, ran the Canadian government up until 2006; all those years, the American military had Khadr in custody, had him at Guantanamo, questioning him, to discover the critical information he knew about al Qaeda's operations in Afghanistan, including his very personal knowledge of friends of the family Osama bin Laden and Ayman al-Zawahiri. And Canadian officials had been questioning him too.

From July 2002, when the United States arrested Omar Khadr for his war crimes, until February 2006, the Canadian government was a Liberal government. In all that time, just a few months shy of four years, and through two different Liberal prime ministers – Jean Chrétien and Paul Martin – the Liberals did nothing, not a single thing, to try to spring Omar Khadr from prison and bring him back to Canada. Quite the contrary. The Liberal government promised Canadians that they would ensure their homegrown al Qaeda soldier was given due process and access to Canadian officials (he was) and that he was being treated humanely (and he was treated amazingly generously). The Liberal foreign affairs minister, Bill Graham, said he was satisfied by assurances from the Red Cross that Khadr was "being properly cared for."[5] Beyond that, the Liberals weren't troubled one bit by the supposed plight of Omar Khadr. In fact, they were severely disinterested. As one report in *The Globe and Mail* summed it up: "The

[Khadr] case was seen as politically untouchable during the dying days of the Jean Chrétien era, and did not emerge as a priority for the Martin government of 2003-2006."[6]

That was when the Liberals actually had the responsibility of running a government, paying attention to the international rules that govern prisoners of war, and had reason to respect the sovereignty of their NATO allies. As the leaders of a significant nation, a party to the War on Terror prosecuted at home and in Afghanistan, and a respected voice in the international community, they also had an obligation to be responsible with the truth. All of that changed when the Liberals lost the 2006 federal election to the Conservatives.

Suddenly out of power, the Liberals began to portray Omar Khadr as a victim of U.S. justice gone amok; a poor "child soldier"[7] deprived of his rights by a merciless hegemon. Irwin Cotler was the minister of justice and attorney general in the Martin government and was almost as internationally renowned as Ignatieff for his erudition when it came to matters of international human rights law. For more than two years, Omar Khadr's detention at Guantanamo "did not emerge as a priority" for Cotler. After the Liberals lost the 2006 election, his job changed from administering justice to assailing his political rivals for their approach to justice – which, in the case of Omar Khadr, was merely a continuation of Cotler's approach. All of sudden Cotler was describing Guantanamo as an "internationally decried" dungeon of "brutality" where Americans used "coercive" measures to unfairly extract dubious confessions from their prisoners.[8] He lacked "confidence," he said, that those immoral American imperialists could be trusted to decide Khadr's fate "through a just process" at Guantanamo. Khadr's "ordeal," he said, was rife with "illegality." Funny he never mentioned it before.

Cotler was delighted when U.S. president Barack Obama was elected: Obama, he said, "prefers to act" more justly than the Conservatives, promising to shut down Guantanamo Bay and "ban torture" there.[9] This should "alter the entire Canadian calculus with respect to the case of Omar Khadr," he decided. Who knows whether Cotler knew that Obama's words, like the Opposition Liberals', were nothing but hollow political grandstanding: like the Liberals, once the president was actually seated in power, and wielded great responsibility, he conceded the necessity – and legitimacy – of Guantanamo, and kept it running, and kept trying war criminals there after all.[10]

Paul Martin decided that saving Omar Khadr from those cruel Americans was a critical issue too – as soon as he stopped being prime minister. In fact, it was under Paul Martin's Liberal government that Omar Khadr was first interrogated by Canadian officials – interrogations that were captured on video but only publicly released years later, under the Conservatives. Stéphane Dion, who succeeded Martin as Liberal leader, even had the gall to write Prime Minister Harper in 2008[11] and complain that he found the interrogation videos – again, the ones made during his own party's reign – "disturbing" and that they suggested "mistreatment." (The tapes, released at the request of his defence lawyers and easily found on YouTube, show Khadr theatrically weeping and lying that he was being harshly treated at Guantanamo while Canadian agents speak to him calmly and patiently – urging him to relax and offering him a hamburger and chocolate bars – while clearly incredulous about his claims of abuse; Khadr makes it clear throughout that what he wants is the officials to bring him back to Canada.[12]) Dion met with Khadr's lawyers personally to express his support and even began complaining that Omar was a "child soldier under the terms of the UN Convention on the Rights of the Child," a fact, he said, that "should never be ignored." Except that – even if that were true (it isn't) – the Liberals were perfectly fine ignoring it during the years they were in charge of the Omar Khadr file.

In fact, Omar Khadr's supporters were furious with the Liberal government for taking that hands-off, we-trust-our-American-allies approach that Professor Michael Ignatieff once elucidated so eloquently. In November 2005, the *Toronto Star* reported that the terrorist's defenders were "appalled" by what they called the "federal government's lack of concern about obtaining even basic concessions" for Khadr, including consular visits, or seeking guarantees that Khadr wouldn't face the death penalty.[13] Dan McTeague, a former Liberal parliamentary secretary who, in the Paul Martin government, was given special responsibility for Canadians detained abroad, waved off the complaints. "We've been given assurances by the Americans that he is being treated in a humane way and we take the Americans at their word."[14] It was going to be "a very long process," requiring patience, he said.[15] Asked about concerns over whether Khadr might face the death penalty, McTeague shrugged: "It's really up to the Americans at this stage."[16] His worry was so minimal, he didn't even find out that the United States had promised to waive the death penalty until reporters informed him of the Americans' decision: "This is news to me," he said at the time.[17] In 2005, Omar's mother complained the Liberals "have not been trying anything," while his Canadian lawyer, Dennis Edney, complained they hadn't even got around to extracting "the most meager concessions" from the Americans on Khadr.[18]

Actually, some Liberals wanted their party to get even tougher than just letting justice take its course with Omar in Guantanamo. In 2004, John Cannis, the MP for Scarborough, home of the Khadr family, sent a letter to Justice Minister Cotler, calling for the whole gang – Omar's mother and siblings – to be charged with "aiding a terrorist organization with which Canada is at war."[19] He knew, as did Ignatieff and so many other Liberals at the time, that al Qaeda types didn't deserve our sympathy but our vigilance. Heck, even the Khadrs knew that: Omar's own brother promised the U.S. news program *60 Minutes* that Omar was just waiting for the chance to get his revenge. "When he's all right again he'll find them again . . . and take his revenge," Kareem Khadr vowed.[20] Cannis sure seemed to get that when he asked

"Are we going to sit back and wait for the bomb to explode before we take action?"

Meantime, Bill Graham, while he was Canada's Liberal foreign minister, said he had assurances from the Red Cross that Khadr was "being properly cared for" in Guantanamo.[21] But that, too, changed once his party was out of power; suddenly, the Liberals decided that the Americans were running a gulag. "If we had known then what we know now, then we would have taken strenuous steps to repatriate Mr. Khadr to Canada. . . . We should have repatriated him, and I believe that we should do it now," Paul Martin told a television interviewer in 2008. Since losing power, Graham and McTeague have trotted out almost the exact same "if only we'd known" line that Martin tried.[22]

But then, as one reporter noted, "Mr. Martin didn't specify . . . what exactly he knows now that he didn't know before" – though the reporter guessed it must have been the "abuse allegations" claimed by Khadr and his supporters. Of course, those were mere allegations (and fairly unbelievable ones). Unlike these folks, the party forming the government has a duty to operate on actual facts.

The Liberals weren't the only ones to suddenly change their tune about Omar Khadr once the Conservatives inherited the file. You'll look hard to find any press releases on Khadr on the website of the group representing Canada's 38,000 lawyers that predate the election of Stephen Harper's Conservative government in 2006; there aren't any. No news stories appear to quote Canada's foremost lawyers' group as being even the slightest bit concerned about Khadr's detention in Guantanamo or his access to justice while the Liberals were in power.

But, since 2006, the Canadian Bar Association (CBA), the men and women who are supposed to represent the pensive face of justice in this country, have issued more press releases devoted to championing an Islamist criminal than they have for everyone else on the planet combined: a search of the CBA website yields 232 items just about one man: Omar Khadr. There are plenty of cases of Canadian citizens who've been imprisoned in foreign countries on thin pretenses. Huseyin Celil, a much more peaceful Muslim than Khadr ever was, is serving a life sentence in China for a string of laughable charges trumped up to paper over the communist country's persecution of him for being a member of the Uyghur minority. Canadian William Sampson was held for three years in a Saudi jail, brutally tortured, forced into a false confession, and sentenced to beheading on bogus charges of coordinating a pair of bombings. To the CBA, Sampson and Celil were nonpersons: they got no press releases calling for their release. No mentions of them on the CBA website at all, actually.

But when Khadr's American defence lawyer stood up at a 2007 CBA conference to hold up Khadr as a "child" who was unfairly treated by the United States and Canada, he got a standing ovation from the audience.[23] Over and over again, the CBA tried pressuring the Conservative government – never the Liberals – demanding that Ottawa repatriate the terrorist to Canada, denying the Americans the right to try him.[24] If the CBA had a general policy of demanding the return of Canadians caught in trouble overseas, its Khadr fetish wouldn't stand out so garishly. But the CBA doesn't. In fact, when it comes to the world's worst regimes, the CBA isn't just silent – it actually helps out in their public rehabilitation.

At the same time that the CBA was condemning the democratic United States of America for its "affront to the rule of law," it was sponsoring a tourist junket for its members to, of all places, Burma. Burma, or Myanmar, as the internationally ostracized governing military junta insists the country should be called, easily ranks as one of the most flagrant human rights abusers on the planet. In 2010, Amnesty International counted twenty-one hundred political prisoners in that country, "the vast majority of which are prisoners of conscience punished merely for peacefully exercising their rights to free expression, assembly and association."[25] There is hardly anything resembling the "rule of law" in Burma, but rather "arbitrary arrest, imprisonment, torture and extra-judicial killing"; "grossly unfair trials, often held inside prisons and lacking defence counsel"; "extremely harsh sentences"; and "prison conditions that fail to meet international standards."

None of that seemed to bother the CBA. Nor did the fact that, at the time it arranged its excursion there – full of sightseeing and shopping – Burma's most prominent democracy activist, Aung San Suu Kyi, a Nobel Peace Prize winner, had just had her house arrest extended. Again. She had been held hostage by the Burmese junta for roughly fifteen years for the crime of leading the

National League for Democracy. Suu Kyi had been fighting for rule of law and basic rights in Burma for decades
and had called on the international community to support
her through a tourism boycott of Burma.[26] But the CBA
went ahead and sent sixty vacationing lawyers there
anyway, on an itinerary that included some great bargains
on lacquerware and rubies.

But the CBA's moral cover for Burma pales next to
its collusion with the Chinese government, another
notorious human rights abuser with its own very pecu-
liar version of the rule of law. According to Amnesty, in
China, "an estimated 500,000 people are currently
enduring punitive detention without charge or trial, and
millions are unable to access the legal system to seek
redress for their grievances."[27] The country is also the
world's most avid executioner, with an estimated "thousands of executions" every year – several times the number
of capital punishments carried out across the rest of the
world combined – though the exact number is not known
because China's idea of a fair and transparent justice
system is to conceal all their killings from the world.

But the CBA doesn't let that stop it from dealing in legal
exchanges with the All China Lawyers Association, a
Communist Party front. If the CBA were meeting with
legal dissidents, or filing lawsuits or petitions on behalf of
political prisoners, that would be one thing. But it's
meeting with lawyers who work for the police state. Not
surprisingly you won't find any mention of the word
Tiananmen on the CBA's website either.

Given the CBA's obvious moral misguidance, it adds up that it would line up behind a terrorist like Omar Khadr without paying mind to the other thousand or so Canadians being detained abroad at any given moment, any number of them surely on far weaker cases and at the mercy of far less trustworthy justice systems than that of the United States of America.

CHAPTER 10

A TAINTED PLEA

Captain Christopher Eason, Office of the
Chief Prosecutor, Office of Military Commissions,
Guantanamo Bay, Cuba: *Ultimately were you able
to come to an opinion regarding the accused's
[Omar Khadr's] risk for future dangerousness?*

Dr. Michael Welner: *I have.*

Capt. Eason: *Please, Doctor, tell us what that opinion is?*

Dr. Welner: *He is highly dangerous.*

> Testimony of forensic psychiatrist Dr. Michael Welner,
> chairman of the Forensic Panel, sentencing hearing for
> Omar Khadr, October 26, 2010

L ee Boyd Malvo must be wondering why he couldn't have got himself an army lawyer. Malvo was the teenager arrested in October 2002 as the junior member of the Beltway Sniper duo. Along with John Allen Muhammad, aged forty-one, Malvo terrorized Americans for three harrowing weeks that year as the two of them skulked around Maryland, Virginia, and Washington, D.C., in a modified Chevrolet Caprice designed so they could fire an assault rifle from the trunk. They shot thirteen people, one a middle-schooler, killing ten of them. This was less than three months after Omar Khadr attacked a group of Americans in Khost, Afghanistan. Like Omar Khadr, Malvo was a minor – just seventeen at the time of his arrest. Like Omar Khadr, Malvo pled guilty to the attacks. Unlike Omar Khadr, Malvo was sentenced to six consecutive life terms – one for each murder he confessed to – without the possibility of parole.

It's true that Omar Khadr confessed to just one murder. No one knows for sure how many he committed in total, though at Guantanamo, custodial records noted him to be "bragging to guards about how many Americans he had killed."[1] A video recovered at the Khost al Qaeda compound where Khadr killed army medic Christopher Speer showed Khadr cheerfully assembling landmines designed to kill American and Canadian troops. No one knows how many times Khadr had shot and killed NATO forces before that 2002 day in Khost. For all Khadr's claims of torture and harsh interrogation methods, a forensic psychiatrist hired to review Khadr noted that the teenaged terrorist was extremely careful – and clever – in avoiding any discussions of any previous attacks he might have been involved in.

For the only murder he was charged with, Omar Khadr was sentenced by a jury to forty years in prison.

But not really.

The jury thought they were giving Omar Khadr forty years. This was a jury panel carefully selected by Omar Khadr's defence team from across the U.S. armed forces: Khadr's Canadian lawyer, Dennis Edney, hired Joe Guastaferro, a "trial consultant" who advertises that he offers his lawyer clients a "persuasion advantage" by helping select the right jury to provide the right "perception of the facts."[2] The defence had the right to challenge any potential juror – and have them removed – if it can claim to have cause to.[3] Meanwhile, although prosecutors appealed to the judge to exclude potential jurors who believed that the detainee prison at Guantanamo should be shut down altogether, or because they believed the U.S. government's definition of *torture* was too narrow (and so believed the government permitted torture) – suggesting this exhibited a "hostile attitude" toward government policies – the presiding judge, Patrick Parrish, rejected the prosecution's challenges.[4] Some said the jury was effectively "handpicked" for the defence – one trial witness said the judge was "smacking down the prosecution's challenges" of potential jurors "and granting the defense's challenges."[5] Still, that "handpicked" jury found Omar Khadr guilty and sentenced him to forty years in prison.[6]

But not really.

What the jury didn't know is that Omar Khadr's trial was a sham. When Khadr's supporters in the media and on Canadian university campuses promised that he'd get only a "show trial," designed, as *Toronto Star* columnist Thomas Walkom put it, for "public relations,"[7] they can't have meant this. But they were right: this was, quite literally, a show trial. The jury's verdict, it turned out, was entirely meaningless. Omar Khadr, tried by the army he had sworn to kill, defended by soldiers he had vowed to defeat, prosecuted by the very people he had built bombs to destroy, was allowed to ignore the jury's verdict. He was given a deal. It was possibly the most bizarre, most generous deal the United States ever bestowed upon an al Qaeda terrorist with American blood on his hands. It was coordinated right out of the White House: the Obama administration ordered prosecutors to sign on the dotted line. It was an "extraordinary last minute intervention by U.S. Secretary of State Hillary Clinton aimed at resolving a case that was becoming an embarrassment for the Obama administration," as MSNBC national correspondent Michael Isikoff described it.[8]

"While U.S. military prosecutors were anxious to proceed with the trial and lay out their case against Khadr, the White House and the State Department were anxious to avoid any further proceedings against the defendant . . . [due to] fierce international criticism that President Barack Obama's administration was prosecuting – as the first case before its new and revamped military commissions – a detainee who was a teenager at the time he committed his alleged offenses," Isikoff reported. Clinton called up Canadian foreign affairs minister Lawrence Cannon and asked if Canada would be willing to consider taking Khadr off their hands if they handed him a light sentence. Cannon agreed. Khadr would have to serve a minimum of just one more year in U.S. custody before the Americans would allow him to apply for transfer to Canada, where, based on his time served, he will likely be eligible for parole almost immediately.

A Pentagon source reveals that the order came down from the highest levels at the White House and Department of Defense. Khadr's defence strategy had fallen apart: his claims of torture were found to be bogus and so all his incriminating statements were permitted by the judge into evidence; the defence team's plan to argue that evidence showed that Khadr was too badly wounded and disabled to have possibly thrown the grenade was demolished by the first witness, who pointed out that the badly wounded man in the photo that they presented as evidence wasn't actually Khadr, but another, dead terrorist (he had a beard).

The Obama administration itself was long "uncomfortable" prosecuting a murder committed by a fifteen-year-old, says the source. Prosecutors were well on their way to building a strong case for why precisely Khadr deserved to be tried as an adult for the murder of Christopher Speer, by proving that Khadr had demonstrated independent thinking, Jihadist motivation, and homicidal intent toward Americans well before he chose to fight and to kill Christopher Speer. But just when momentum started to shift strongly in their favour and toward a conviction, the Obama administration jumped in and demanded prosecutors strike a deal. "It was like somebody running for a touchdown, completely untouched, and the coach from his own side runs and tackles him," says the source. The defence team, aware that the Obama administration was putting pressure on its own prosecutors team, held out for the best deal they could get – which is what they got.

"The Obama administration jammed the plea deal down the prosecutor's throats," said Sgt. Layne Morris, who took part in the battle with Omar Khadr's al Qaeda crew and, in the process, lost his right eye – and his comrade Christopher Speer. "For as long as I have known the prosecutor he has insisted that there was not going to be a deal since they had a great case."[9] And then the Obama administration got involved.

Despite all the evidence against Khadr, and the disintegration of his two main lines of defence, Khadr's lawyers were given the advantage over the prosecutors by decree of the Obama administration. And Canada's foreign minister, Lawrence Cannon, played along.

President Obama and Lawrence Cannon decided that Canada's neighbourhoods were a better home for an avowed, unrepentant, unreformed, gleeful Islamic terrorist than the facility at Guantanamo Bay. Lee Boyd Malvo must have wish he'd been so lucky as to have been a sworn terrorist from al Qaeda caught building bombs to blow up U.S. soldiers, shooting at translators and troops, and tossing a grenade to murder an army medic in Afghanistan, instead of asleep in a modified Chevy at a rest stop on Maryland's Interstate 70.

Hard as it might be to believe, it could have been worse: Khadr's deal was so sweet that Washington allowed the trial to play out in case the jury came back with an even lighter sentence. "In other words, Khadr could roll the dice and get the better of the two sentences," reported Elise Cooper from the Conservative website FrumForum.com.[10] Had the jury come back with a sentence of just seven, or six, or even three years, Khadr's deal with prosecutors would be cancelled, and he'd get the lighter sentence offered from the jury. Except, even a jury specially arranged for the defence team's "persuasion advantage," comprised of several people opposed in principle to Guantanamo Bay and the interrogation methods used on some prisoners there, couldn't stomach the idea of giving Omar Khadr just eight years, only one of them required to be served in Gitmo. Even prosecutors only asked for Khadr to get sixteen years, but the jury, after hearing all the evidence, went beyond that and sentenced Khadr to four decades in the brig. Only, by then, their opinion didn't count anymore. The politicians had made their decision. The show trial was tossed aside. The admitted terrorist was let go. All because it made the Obama administration feel more comfortable – even if it ends up making Canadians, who will be forced to live alongside the al Qaeda murderer, a lot less so.

Those jurors believed Omar Khadr deserved to stay in prison until he'd hit retirement age. In part, that's because those jurors knew something about Khadr that few Canadians did, information they heard from Dr. Michael Welner.

Dr. Michael Welner, an associate professor of psychiatry at New York University's School of Medicine and adjunct professor at Duquesne University School of Law, is surely the top forensic psychiatrist in the United States. He's been called to testify in five other military trials, two involving members of al Qaeda – including Mamdouh Salim, an original co-founder of al Qaeda charged with organizing a series of bombing attacks against U.S. embassies in East Africa in 1998 – and has testified as an expert witness roughly a hundred times in civilian trials. He's acted as a key forensic psychiatry consultant on some of America's most notorious criminal cases: the infamous 1998 murder of Matthew Shepard, allegedly targeted for being gay; the 2006 trial of Andrea Yates, who murdered her five children by drowning them in her bathtub; the

2007 investigation into the murder-suicide committed by pro wrestling star Chris Benoit; the case of the man who kidnapped fourteen-year-old Elizabeth Smart in 2002 and held her prisoner for nine months; and many other cases, both high profile and less famous. The president of the six-thousand-member American Academy of Forensic Sciences has praised Dr. Welner's "meticulous" work and his reports' "amazing quality of detail."[11] Dr. Welner personally developed the "Depravity Scale," a tool developed for forensic psychiatrists to standardize the language around crimes distinguished by their cruelty or brutality. Dr. Welner sits on a panel, appointed by the New York State Court, that evaluates the risk of recidivism in prisoners being considered for release. In 1997, he was honoured by the thirty-eight-thousand-member American Psychiatric Association with the Award of Excellence in Medical Student Education, and he contributed a chapter to the FBI's *Crime Classification Manual*. As founder and chairperson of the Forensic Panel, America's first peer-reviewed forensic psychiatry consultancy (meaning it is the first held up to rigorous scientific standards), he oversees fifty specialists in the field.[12]

The Pentagon hired Dr. Welner to do a forensic psychiatric analysis of Omar Khadr to determine how dangerous Khadr would be if he were released from prison, part of which required understanding whether Khadr was indeed just a young naïf, press-ganged into the service of al Qaeda, as his apologists have always claimed, or instead a devoted and remorseless terrorist, as prosecutors alleged.

Dr. Welner personally interviewed Khadr for eight hours in Guantanamo Bay. He reviewed nearly 150 sources in more than 500 hours of research on Khadr – sources that included legal documents, reports from medical personnel, transcripts and videos of Khadr's interrogations, Khadr's letters to his family and friends, and personal interviews with guards and interrogators at Guantanamo. Dr. Welner put together the most thorough, most expert forensic analysis of Khadr's mental state that anyone could possibly ask for. His final report to prosecutors stretched more than sixty pages.

Dr. Welner's analysis was, almost certainly, what Khadr's lawyers, and President Obama, feared the most. And with good reason: what Dr. Welner discovered was, to say the least, alarming. Defence lawyers fought desperately to keep the videotape of Dr. Welner's interview with Khadr out of evidence. And even though the jury requested to see it, Khadr's defence team succeeded. They fought desperately to keep Dr. Welner's final report out of the hands of the jury. Again, they succeeded.

But they couldn't keep Dr. Welner off the stand altogether. And had the jurors actually seen Dr. Welner's report or that videotape, they might have handed Khadr a far harsher sentence than the forty years they ended up giving him. What Dr. Welner discovered was nothing like the victimized ingénue "child soldier" defence attorneys and supporters tried to paint Khadr as. Instead, he found Khadr to be a precocious, sly, calculating man who had played the Americans very carefully from the moment he was captured and who did not for a moment exhibit any regret for the bloodshed and mayhem he had deliberately and eagerly set out to cause.

From the start, Dr. Welner's analysis showed that Khadr was different than other al Qaeda terrorists taken into custody, even ones older than he. He was "less frightened and . . . needed less reassurance" from the medical staff who treated him at Bagram Air Base after he was rescued from the compound in Khost.[13] He was "not as distressed as other teenagers" based on reports from surprised medical staff. Instead, "he was smiling a lot" and "quite jovial with doctors, always trying to engage others." This was the first sign of the remarkable charm and ease – documented at length in Dr. Welner's report – that Khadr was able to employ to win support and sympathy. It's little wonder that so many gullible journalists, lawyers, and other dupes fell for it.

Dr. Welner noted that in a video discovered in the Khost compound, showing Khadr assembling landmines to be used to blow up North American soldiers, he was clearly "excitedly looking forward to killing Americans." Unlike most child soldiers, who are drugged to force them to comply with wartime atrocities, Khadr was never once in his life under the influence of drugs or narcotics, Dr. Welner noted. He was nothing like typical child soldiers. Rather, while Khadr built his instruments of death and destruction, he showed only a "smiling, enthusiastic, and relaxed attitude." There was, says Dr. Welner, "not a whit of evidence of Omar Khadr's discomfort with his activities in the home [where the bombs were being assembled] or with his peers in the home."[14]

And unlike so many terrorists, jihadis, and allied soldiers who have been through the most traumatic wartime experiences – among which, being trapped in a compound being bombed into rubble while your fellow soldiers are slaughtered one by one must surely rank quite high – Khadr amazingly never displayed any sign of posttraumatic stress disorder (PTSD), Dr. Welner noted. "Mr. Khadr is more defined by his resilience than by signs of PTSD" that might have, in a weaker spirit, been caused by "his experiences in battle, his life threatening injuries, or the carnage he witnessed before capture."[15]

Nor did Khadr seem to experience anything by way of sleeping difficulties. He "denied intrusive recollections or thoughts." His nightmares were, as with many of us who haven't fought in terrorist attacks, merely "occasional." When he was interrogated about the brutal and bloody firefight at Khost – men getting their heads shot off, limbs being blown off – Dr. Welner found that Khadr "was not sweating or hyperventilating as if in a state of hyperarousal" but rather was "thoughtful and reflecting." He never required, or asked for, psychiatric counselling. Khadr later admitted that on the one occasion when he seemed depressed, and even suicidal, he had been playing up his homesickness to "try to gain phone call privileges."[16] It was all a fraud.

Khadr wasn't troubled by what he did in Afghanistan. He wasn't even haunted by what must have been the most horrific scenes of violence and blood and gore and death. Rather, Dr. Welner noted, he apparently "bragged" about it to his fellow inmates in Guantanamo. The spoiled prince of al Qaeda made himself a "rock star," to quote a Gitmo guard, among the other prisoners who were in awe of his war stories and his family's place in the upper echelons of the world's most vicious and dangerous terror network. More than that, his "access to many attorneys volunteering for him and to sympathetic media" looked to the other inmates – who didn't enjoy the benefit of the cheerleading squad that Khadr had – like "a conduit through which they can advance their cause." To the other inmates at Guantanamo – men going all the way up to the highest levels of the world's terrorist hierarchy – Khadr became their kingpin, Dr. Welner realized. Having memorized the Koran, and regularly leading their prayers, he has, it seems, become their spiritual guide too: Khadr distinguished himself, as the ecstatic murderer had always hoped to, as the biggest, smartest, most deadly fish in a pond teeming with the most vicious, depraved men on Earth.

And he knew it. As Dr. Welner noted in his report, Khadr was a man with a great sense of entitlement and grandeur. Khadr has "cultivated assets" in the "sympathetic news media . . . who fuel the mantra of his convicted murderer being a victim of justice." He speaks to military guards with the "air of an employer and with the subtle refinement of a person of important self-esteem." Welner discovered that Khadr had taken to calling a female, African-American military guard "bitch," "whore," and, most appallingly, "slave."[17] It was as if they were his inferior servants, there only to serve his whims. In fact, when they did, such as providing him with special forms of entertainment or comfort, he refused to share these with his fellow inmates, apparently so beneath him, even when encouraged to by guards. "Let them ask for their own," he'd say.[18] The prince of al Qaeda, it seems, doesn't share with common terrorist foot soldiers. Dr. Welner found him to exhibit the "entitlement of narcissism, or [of a] spoiled celebrity."[19]

Khadr told Dr. Welner that he had grown up "the favourite child" of the al Qaeda family. "His best sense of this is his personality," Dr. Welner reported. "He characterizes himself as easygoing and with a 'very, very cool temper.'" For all his lawyers' claims of the miserable mistreatment Khadr had experienced at Gitmo, a study of Khadr showed he would "characterize himself as happy." In fact, when Dr. Welner tried to dig into Khadr's claims of torture, he discovered a prisoner who seemed curiously uninterested in talking about it. It was, as Dr. Welner said, as though Khadr was so bored and tired of these tales of torture, he couldn't bother himself to get into them.[20] He waved Dr. Welner off and told him that if he really wanted to know, he should go look it all up in the court documents.

"Asked to recount his experiences, the defendant repeatedly asserts that he was tortured and abused to the current day," Dr. Welner wrote in his report. "When asked to detail such torture, he refers me to his affidavit as if he is otherwise unable to recall details. . . . Mr. Khadr uses the affidavit" – in other words, his lawyers' assertions and not his own version of events – "as a substitute for a personal narrative. He dispatches my probing of his allegations with a disdain that he should not have to bother discussing this."[21] Dr. Welner said, "He referred me to the affidavit of his case with the ennui of a person who did not want to be bothered with the details. He was more annoyed that I would take the time to explore what was asserted, with great consternation, in his affidavit."[22]

That is nothing less than astonishing. Khadr enthusiastically detailed for Dr. Welner how he would place his landmines, how precisely, to the metre, they must be spaced in order to ensure maximum impact on the targeted American troops, but seems "unable to recall details" of this supposedly traumatic torture that occurred over months and months. When the subject is killing Americans, Khadr can't wait to brag at length all about his exploits. When he's pressed to divulge all the supposedly terrible things that have been done to his body and his mind, all the terrible injustices committed against him, he gets annoyed, as if it's the least important thing anyone could be discussing with him.

Khadr's stories about torture were never found to be true, of course: his journalist fan club credulously ran with the stories about Khadr being dropped hard on his injuries, or forced to wet himself and then used by guards as a human mop to clean it up, suffocated, or short-shackled for hours on end, as if they were fact. But there was never any evidence of torture other than Khadr's reports. There was scarcely any evidence of mistreatment of prisoners at Guantanamo Bay, period. But let's think how someone might react if they were, in fact, tortured by guards. You'd imagine they'd be eager to tell someone, anyone, but particularly a psychiatrist, about it. Someone who's been tortured would want the world to know about it. William Sampson, the Canadian dual citizen falsely imprisoned by Saudi Arabia from 2000 to 2003, continually and persistently told anyone who would listen about the torture used to extract his false confession of being linked to a bombing in Riyadh. Sampson eventually wrote a book about it – *Confessions of an Innocent Man: Torture and Survival in a Saudi Prison*. He later even tried suing his torturers.[23] Understandably, the torture he experienced became a fixation for Sampson, as it would presumably for anyone who'd been through it. He was, as any torture victim would be, scarred by it for life.

Sampson was tortured until he confessed to a crime he didn't commit. In fact, one of the most common and difficult criticisms of torture as an interrogation device is that it's often as likely to provoke a false confession "as a means of escaping the stresses of an interrogation" as it is to elicit a genuine one.[24]

But Dr. Welner made an interesting discovery when he analyzed how Khadr responded to his own interrogations, even those allegedly employing harsh and painful treatment.

He told them nothing.

In other words, even if Khadr was subjected to harsh methods, it didn't work. Not one bit. Indeed, there is plenty in Dr. Welner's report to disprove all the far-fetched claims of torture. It took sixty-five hours of visits from a psychologist working for Khadr's own defence team – a sympathetic ear if ever there was one – for Khadr to even think to mention anything about torture.[25] He never mentioned any torture in letters to his family.[26] There was no sign in his medical records of any injuries that might have resulted from abuse or torture.[27] These were just lies, made up – as al Qaeda's training manual advises – to win sympathy and weaken the case against him. When Dr. Welner asked, "What interrogation techniques most approximated torture to him," Khadr told him it was "threats of rape" – stories allegedly told by the interrogators about big dangerous men at Guantanamo and other prisons that would sodomize him if he didn't come clean. For all his lawyers' insistence that Khadr was physically abused, the worst form of "torture" to Omar Khadr was dark warnings about what might happen to him in prison. And even then, Dr. Welner noted, "it did not elicit self-incriminating statements."[28]

That Khadr referred to these scare tactics as "torture" demonstrates just how ready he was to throw that term around, at anything and everything he didn't like. He told Dr. Welner it was like "torture" when one interrogator screamed at him. He told him it was "torture" being kept a prisoner. And Khadr called it "torture" to have to watch the videotape showing him putting landmines together.[29] And yet, in reality, Dr. Welner discovered that his captors had treated Khadr exceptionally gently. "So sensitive to him were the interviewers that just the out-of-character sight of Omar Khadr crying triggered an immediate termination of questioning and concerted psychiatric workup," he noted.[30] Khadr "emphasizes every sense of American misstep, real and illusory, as abuse and torture," Dr. Welner added. He was prone to the "banal flipping around of the words 'torture' and 'abuse.'"[31] "It is my professional opinion that the affidavit he submitted demonstrates his determination to do and say whatever he believes he must in order to help his case," Dr. Welner concluded.[32]

In fact, far from fearing so-called harsh methods of interrogation or torture, Khadr, it turns out, seemed to enjoy the interrogations. He showed a "remarkable . . . lack of fear" when speaking to interrogators, Dr. Welner noted. He even asked one of his interrogators who had believed he had no more information to offer, "Why are you not coming to interview me?" He "openly requested to be able to speak with her whenever possible."[33] When visited by Guantanamo Bay's psychologists in 2003, Khadr told them he "would not mind staying here at GTMO because it's not so bad."[34] Hardly the words of someone being brutally mistreated.

Khadr began by using a false name. "He did not even disclose his name in spite of interrogation techniques that raised his fears," Dr. Welner noted.[35] It took him till his fifth interrogation just to admit he was from Canada. He was "a liar, evasive, knew more than what he let us know," in the words of one interrogator. There was "little actionable intelligence" gleaned from Khadr's questionings – until his eleventh interview.[36]

That was when U.S. authorities showed him the video they had found: the one recovered at the al Qaeda compound Khadr had been holed up in, showing him gleefully assembling landmines and gushing about how excited he is to murder Americans. Before then, Khadr had kept mum. He wasn't involved in al Qaeda, he maintained. He was just a lowly translator, a go-between, caught in the wrong place at the wrong time. "The defendant indicated that he had been lying to his American interrogators until they showed him the bomb-making video."[37]

"The video opened the floodgates," recalled one interrogator.[38] Only when Khadr had been caught "with his hand in the cookie jar," as one interrogator put it, did he finally start admitting to his key role in the al Qaeda cell, building explosives, targeting Americans, shooting and throwing grenades at Christopher Speer's unit. "Mr. Khadr endured 42 interrogations in 90 days. He did not implicate himself in bomb-making activities until shown the video" and even then, only "after many interviews," Dr. Welner reported.[39]

Khadr, it turns out, was an incredibly tough nut to crack. In the face of the most advanced psychological interrogation methods deployed by what must be the sharpest, most well-trained guards on the planet, he wouldn't give up anything. That's not the kind of personality you'd expect from a "child soldier." It's not the kind of thing Guantanamo guards expect even from their most recalcitrant terrorist inmates. Omar Khadr was an exceptional al Qaeda terrorist, even in captivity.

In fact, when Dr. Welner met Khadr, he was struck by the terrorist's canniness and by how adept he was at exploiting situations to his advantage. From the beginning, Khadr was busy calculating how to use Dr. Welner to help himself. "His responses and comportment demonstrated a self-assurance with which he could advance his own interests through the vehicle of our encounter," Dr. Welner remarked. His "pauses to calculate self-serving answers were gaping" – taking the time to come up with just the right responses to benefit himself. He became "anxious and irritable when the interview is more difficult for him to control," Dr. Welner noted. And when Khadr didn't like certain questions – "uncomfortable" ones about his own, and his family's, terrorist activities – he demanded to know why they were being asked, "with an entitlement . . . asserting his 'right' to know." When Dr. Welner wouldn't say, Khadr went a step further, seeming to suggest subtly to Dr. Welner that the doctor might soon find himself accused of abuse or torture as well. He was "quick to suggest . . . that I should not want to 'cause your patient harm and pain' by probing such issues, doing so with a faint smirk," Dr. Welner reported.[40]

Dr. Welner was struck by Khadr's skill in manipulating the interview to suit his own purposes. "He coolly dispatches questions with non-answers or claims not to remember, with the occasional detail alternating with the implausible. His responses are such departures from the available record that his ability to carry it off as much as he does is impressive as well," Dr. Welner wrote. "When his evasiveness does not evade, he confidently endeavors to place the examiner on the defensive by posing his own questions to take over the interview, or by invoking 'human rights.' This, of course, is a very effective technique when one has to communicate with a self-effacing and universalist Westerner, all too ready to scurry into guilt when challenged about human rights and the Geneva Convention by a person whose confederates were flaunting beheadings of everyone from care givers to aid workers to journalists. But it is that brazenness to seek out debate that reflects Omar Khadr's strength – and [it's] a brazenness many adults don't have."[41]

Omar Khadr was widely presented in boosterish news reports in Canada as a hopelessly lost child, victimized by so many terrible people, from his family, to the Canadian government, to the U.S. military. Dr. Welner's examination shows just how badly all those journalists were played for fools by a young terrorist more clever, and more devious, than they. Dr. Welner's objective and scientific analysis revealed a side of Khadr they were never able, or wouldn't allow themselves, to see, blinded as they were with bias against the Bush administration and the War on Terror generally.

One particularly stunning incident that Dr. Welner noted in his report shows just how cunningly Khadr played the gullible journalists: one morning, when Dr. Welner was visiting Guantanamo Bay, he noticed Khadr wearing a sling to court that day, "complaining of shoulder pain." Later that same day, as the doctor received a tour of Guantanamo from guards there, he ran into Khadr again.

The sling was gone. The pain, too, evidently, was gone. "Mr. Khadr emerged from the television room . . . walked over to engage the group in a friendly manner, waving his arms and without any apparent limitation in range of motion in his shoulder – and without a sling. Later that evening, he joined his peers for a game of soccer." So, when the *Toronto Star*'s soft-hearted reporter Michelle Shephard is around – she who describes Khadr as "an awkward puppy"[42] and who couldn't shake how "despondent" he looked at trial[43] – he is smart enough to play wounded. When she's not around, he plays soccer.

Dr. Welner had it nailed: Omar Khadr had a brazenness that just didn't compute in the minds of the credulous, upper-middle-class Westerners who tried to figure him out. He'd been reared in a world of deception: his father's entire career was based on lying to donors about orphans in Afghanistan while funnelling their money to his terrorist partners. He watched his mother manipulate the prime minister of Canada to get his dad off of a terrorist charge. To Khadr, "human rights" were meaningless on the battlefield, where his friends shot the heads off translators and he blew up a medic while he searched for the wounded, but they were useful tools to be exploited in the courtroom to hoodwink dupable journalists. Even his interrogators at Guantanamo, used to interrogating al Qaeda's usual, unworldly cannon fodder, were hardly much of a match for the sly and scheming Khadr, Dr. Welner determined. "Omar Khadr came into custody with the *je ne sais quoi* to parry interrogators like the callow young

American louts who regaled him with tales about American prisons as they would the crude dead-enders they were used to dealing with. And parry them he did." He "cultivated relationships" with interrogators "who were taken in by his age and sweet smile."[44] After all, concluded Dr. Welner, "what is it to be spooked by some foul military interrogators with ugly tattoos when you have hung out with bomb-makers who banally spurt blood from the deformed hand of a person who didn't get the bomb-assembly right?"[45]

As Dr. Welner would later write to Vice Admiral Bruce MacDonald, the Pentagon official overseeing the tribunals at Guantanamo: "Omar Khadr is not a child soldier in the manner that has afflicted so many conflicts. He was never uprooted from his family, never desensitized to violence with drugs and alcohol, never groomed into violence from a peaceful origin. He glorified violence rather than was horrified by it (as are child soldiers). Khadr was a worldly 15-year-old rather than a naïve one. His family supported his violence, rather than adopting it from captors' influence. Child soldiers seek nothing. Omar Khadr sought martyrdom."[46] Omar Khadr had spent his whole, young life seeking to distinguish himself from his fellow al Qaeda terrorists as someone special. He was. According to Dr. Welner, Khadr was distinct in that, unlike some al Qaeda captives, he was "highly dangerous."[47]

It's no coincidence that of every public assertion available from those who came into direct contact with Khadr – the U.S. soldiers, the guards at Guantanamo, the psychiatrists who examined him, and finally the jury at the Guantanamo tribunal – only his defence lawyers claimed to believe anything different. Meanwhile, journalists like Michelle Shephard, who never did have contact with Khadr and, blinkered by their gullibility, their guilty Western consciences, and their inability to see Khadr as anything but a young man from a Toronto neighbourhood just like theirs, spun a story that, as is now evident thanks to Dr. Welner's thorough analysis, was completely detached from the very chilling, highly dangerous reality that is Omar Khadr.

Khadr's lawyers hired several psychologists of their own. But in the end, they didn't testify or try to rebut Dr. Welner's testimony. It's hard to put a pleasant spin on a psychopathic terrorist who confessed to the joy he felt in murdering a man. And so, Dr. Welner's condemnation went completely unrebutted.

And thanks to their foolishness and the irresponsible stories they used to foment angst over the Khadr case among the Canadian public and internationally, this remorseless, manipulative, and highly dangerous terrorist won't serve the forty-year sentence that a fair-minded and, most importantly, informed military jury believed he merited. Instead, he will likely be free and roaming Canadian streets before he's even thirty years old.

CHAPTER 11

THE GUANTANAMO TRAINING ACADEMY

"In early 2000, Omar Khadr traveled to the front lines with an al Qaeda cleric named Sheikh Issa. Sheikh Issa was a scholar for al Qaeda who answered questions about the Koran. Khadr indicated that Sheikh Issa also taught a class in Kabul. In the class, students learned the rules for Jihad, including: (1) What to do if one captures a spy – hang him; (2) What to do if one captures a Muslim soldier – kill him; (3) One is allowed to take the weapon from an enemy soldier whom one killed; and (4) Americans were non-believers and it was justified to kill them."

Confession of Omar Ahmed Khadr, October 13, 2010

On December 25, 2009, Umar Farouk Abdulmutallab attempted murder on 279 civilians when he boarded Northwest Airlines Flight 253 from Amsterdam to Detroit, Michigan, with his underpants full of explosives. As we know, a mass murder was narrowly avoided, thanks to a defectively fired detonator and some plucky passengers and crew with sufficient presence of mind and nerve to apprehend the smouldering terrorist, extinguish his fuse, and tie him down for the rest of the harrowing flight. Most of us have also heard about the numerous security and intelligence flaws that failed in the weeks, and even hours, leading up to the aborted attack: Abdulmutallab's father had alerted the CIA in November about his son's intensifying militantism, but the agency neglected to add his name to the no-fly list or look into revoking his U.S. visa (British security officials had already placed Abdulmutallab on their own no-fly list and revoked his British visa); plus, he had paid for his $3,000 ticket in cash and boarded a transatlantic flight with no luggage, both bright red flags.[1]

But there was one critical security failure that didn't get nearly as much mention in the analysis and political aftermath of the Christmas Day attack: that the origins of the plot could be traced back to, of all places, the American-run prison at Guantanamo Bay.

The plan to commit what, had it succeeded, would have ranked as the largest terrorist attack on America since 9/11 may not necessarily have been hatched at Guantanamo Bay. But a key man behind the underwear bombing attack did, it turns out, spend time at Guantanamo. He was Prisoner #372, Said Ali Shari.[2] He was there for six years. And, amazingly, he was released back to the Mideast, where he would continue to pursue the holy war against Westerners – to become one of the four men suspected in leading the planning of the Flight 253 bombing plot.[3] Like Omar Khadr, he claimed he had nothing to do with militant Islam. He was "just a Muslim and not a terrorist," he told the Guantanamo review board that approved his release in 2007.[4] The United States had him; the United States let him go; the United States almost paid for that decision with the lives of nearly three hundred people.

Shari was even sent to Saudi Arabia in 2007 as a candidate eligible to take part in the Saudis' terrorist "rehabilitation" program.[5] It evidently didn't do much good. Perhaps that's not surprising, since the program consists of something called "art therapy," where terrorists are encouraged to use crayons and fingerpaints to get their "negative energy out on paper." They also get perks like a new car and a home if they promise to behave. Even a wife.[6] Sounds a little like kindergarten but with bigger rewards – and bigger behavioural problems. For men who think they'll get seventy-two virgins in the afterlife if they die in a blaze of infidel-killing glory, a Toyota Yaris and a two-bedroom apartment in Riyadh will probably do little to convince them to change their murderous ways. What's truly scary is that the Saudi government claims to have "rehabilitated" more than seven hundred al Qaeda terrorists this way. Just the same, you might be wise to steer clear of their alumni get-togethers.

Shari didn't stay in Saudi Arabia, though. After hanging up his crayons, he headed for Yemen, where he became a key leader in the al Qaeda division based there – the number-two man, actually, in a country where, as a *Jerusalem Post* analysis puts it, "the most active branch of the terror movement, al-Qaida in the Arabian Peninsula, is based."[7] Before the attack on Northwest flight 253, and just a year after his release, Shari was tied to a bombing attack on the U.S. Embassy in Sana.[8]

In fact, al Qaeda in Yemen has become something of a magnet for ex-Guantanamo inmates: there are estimated to be half a dozen or more former U.S. prisoners of war who have arrived there via Guantanamo Bay and are now helping to dream up more plans to bomb American targets and spill Westerners' blood. The Obama administration has finally put a stop to releasing any more Guantanamo inmates[9] because it believes that there's too big a chance that more of them will make for the failing state of Yemen and "return to the fight," as the official phrasing goes. In other words, they'll become active al Qaeda terror soldiers once again. After promising up and down that he would close Guantanamo Bay once elected president, Barack Obama realized, once in power, just how dangerous the men inside that prison were and how perilous it would be to release them upon the world again.

Unfortunately, that new, tougher policy line comes far too late. For years, thanks to ongoing pressure from Western liberal groups and journalists out to shame Washington over Guantanamo, the United States began releasing hundreds of detainees back into the world. It's been a terrible mistake: an astonishing one out of every four detainees has gone back to his terrorist ways. You could fault the George W. Bush administration for setting free such dangerous men, but, to be truly fair, a good deal of that blame actually belongs with the activist groups and journalists who brought so much pressure to bear on the White House over Guantanamo: they're the ones who clamoured that Guantanamo was a horror and that the men there were being unfairly and illegally held – so many of the same people who have demanded the release of Omar Khadr. Even Barack Obama has since awoken to reality and changed his mind. But Omar Khadr's supporters have stuck to their guns. They're perfectly willing to naively believe that Khadr is perfectly safe to let off his leash – even after he's spent years "marinating in a radical jihadist community" at Guantanamo Bay, in the words of Dr. Michael Welner, who conducted the forensic psychiatric analysis of Omar Khadr[10]; immersed in the same terrorist hothouse that graduated the guys behind the Christmas Day bombing. But, unfortunately, Said Ali Shari isn't the only distinguished alumnus of the Guantanamo terror academy.

A report from the U.S. Director of National Intelligence released in December 2010 laid out the sobering statistics of Gitmo's legacy in the most clinical terms. A total of 598 detainees "have been transferred out" of Guantanamo Bay – meaning, released back to their home countries, it said. "The Intelligence Community assesses that 81 (13.5 per cent) are confirmed and 69 (11.5 per cent) are suspected of reengaging in terrorist or insurgent activities after transfer."[11]

Actually, the very fact that they served time in Guantanamo makes them an asset to al Qaeda. The terrorist network considers "recruiting former Guantanamo detainees as great propaganda victories," reports an analysis from the New America Foundation.[12] These are not men writing angry blogs about the United States. These are men returning to hard-core, bloodletting terrorism. These are men returning to take up arms against the United States, Canada, and Europe. And, of course, fellow Muslims they deem to be insufficiently radical.

Mohammed Yusif Yaqub left Guantanamo in 2003 and took over control of all Taliban operations in southern Afghanistan, the very operations Canadian and American troops have been fighting against – and dying from. Abdullah Mehsud, a Pakistani national who insisted to his Gitmo jailers he was but a petty Taliban office clerk and had no interest in terrorism, was let out of Gitmo in March 2004; just a few months later he kidnapped two Chinese engineers working on a dam in Waziristan, one of whom ended up dead, and in 2007 he allegedly helped organize a suicide bombing attack on Pakistan's interior minister that killed thirty-one people. Mohammed al-Awfi, a Saudi, walked out of Guantanamo in November 2007 and turned up not long after as a field commander of al Qaeda's Arabian Peninsula operation in Yemen. Abdullah Ghulam Rasoul is now reputed to be a top deputy of Taliban leader Mullah Omar's, in charge of the organization in southern Afghanistan; he was let out of Guantanamo in 2007. Abdul Rauf Aliza became an aid to another one of Omar's top deputies after he returned to Afghanistan from Guantanamo in 2007. Hani al Shulan of Yemen is now an al Qaeda field commander in his home country. The Saudi Ibrahim Sulayman Muhammad Arbaysh found work as the "theological guide" to al Qaeda in the Arabian Peninsula after leaving Guantanamo in 2006.

Hafizullah Shabaz Khail went home to Afghanistan after serving time in Guantanamo, in 2007, and started attacking U.S. forces, including a reported rocket attack on an American base in 2007. The Pakistani Sha Mohammed Alikhel was released from Guantanamo in 2003 and wound up dead after attacking U.S. forces in Afghanistan for the Taliban. Abdulla Majid Al Naimi, a Bahraini let out of Guantanamo in 2005, was recaptured three years later in Saudi Arabia for being "involved in terrorist facilitations." Ibrahim Shafir Sen went back to Turkey after his 2003 release from Guantanamo to lead an al Qaeda cell in his home country. Zahir Shah is still at large; since leaving Guantanamo in 2007, the Afghani has been actively arranging "terrorist training" back home. Moroccans Mohammed

Bin Ahmad Mizouz and Ibrahim Bin Shakaran both returned home to recruit fighters for ál Qaeda in Iraq after departing Guantanamo on the same day in 2004. The Kuwaiti Abdallah Salih al-Ajmi didn't live long after he left Guantanamo in 2005; he detonated himself in a suicide truck bombing in Iraq in 2008 that reportedly killed thirteen Iraqi policemen and injured forty-two others. Mohammed Ismail, of Afghanistan, left Guantanamo in January 2004; within four months, he was recaptured, caught attacking U.S. forces in Kandahar. Mohammed Ilyas of Pakistan is thought to have led the bombing of an Italian restaurant in front of the Danish Embassy in Pakistan as well as a bombing that killed the Pakistan Army Surgeon General in 2008; he was released from U.S. custody in 2004. The Jordanian Usama Hassan Ahmed Abu Kabir took advantage of his freedom after being let out of U.S. custody in 2007 to plan attacks against Israel.

Not only Arabs and East Asians have gone back to their old ways: Ravil Gumarov and Timur Ishmurat, a pair of Russians held in Guantanamo, were re-arrested back home a year after their release for bombing a gas line.[13]

As alarming as this list may seem, this is just a small sample of all the jihadis who walked out of Guantanamo to take up arms against the Western world. What's even more chilling is that the Director of National Intelligence figures – and with good reason – that the rate of terrorists returning to al Qaeda is an underestimation. Intelligence analyses indicate "that the number of former detainees identified as reengaged in terrorist activity will increase," it reports, because reports of a prisoner's return to the al Qaeda jihad usually don't show up for about two and a half years after they're released from custody. So, those prisoners released in the two and a half years before that report was written aren't even turning up yet on Washington's intelligence radar. There were nearly seventy of them.[14]

What did we expect? Guantanamo Bay isn't like normal prisons. Detainees there aren't looking to be scared straight, or find Jesus, or clean up their addiction, or learn a skill that will get them a decent job so they don't have to steal anymore. The men at Gitmo aren't regular prisoners; they're prisoners of war. As long as that war is still being fought, why wouldn't a huge number of them – true believers inculcated in the Islamist cause – immediately return to the fight? These men are soldiers who believe they are on a crusade for Allah that will bring them an eternity of rewards in the afterlife; a few years in a cushy American prison isn't going to convince them to give it all up for a lousy job farming lentils or working at the post office.

This is the crux of a fundamentally flawed conceit about these terrorists. If a man spends his life committing himself to kill infidels in the name of Allah, it hardly figures that being captured, interrogated, and imprisoned by infidels will warm his heart and change his mind. Believing this conceit, as the high rate of Guantanamo recidivism demonstrates, truly is the triumph of hope over experience. Indeed, two of the most influential men in the history of Islamist terror were former inmates captured for their terror-supporting activities. Sayyid Qutb,

the guiding light of the Muslim Brotherhood in Egypt and
the godfather of al Qaeda, was imprisoned in Egypt in
1964 for his radical preaching and links to anti-government
attacks; eight months after he was let out, he was rearrested
for plotting to overthrow the state. One of Qutb's most dedicated and loyal students, Ayman al-Zawahiri, was arrested
as a leader of Egyptian Islamic Jihad after its members
arranged the 1981 assassination of Anwar Sadat. Following
his release, after three years in prison, he would go on to
partner up with Osama bin Laden to create the deadly
terrorist organization al Qaeda.[15]

Dennis Pluchinsky, a longtime U.S. State Department
analyst who's been studying terrorists for more than thirty
years,[16] offers a four-point framework to define someone
who qualifies as a hard-core global jihadist. One, the individual believes that "Islam is under attack by the West with
the objective of destroying Islam"; two, he's convinced the
United States is the primary enemy of Islam; three, he
thinks Islam is destined to rule the world; and, four, his
natural response to the threat against Islam is militant
jihad.[17] Run through the checklist, and with all we know
about Omar Khadr and his family, he hits every single
point. Khadr has had two major stages in his life: his time
spent studying at the school of al Qaeda with his family
and his years at the Guantanamo Bay academy for terrorists. Neither, of course, would have done a single thing to
dissuade him from his hatred of Jews, Christians, and other
infidel Westerners. If anything, both would have nurtured
and honed his hatred more, wouldn't they? Ask his brother,

Kareem – the one who eagerly promised 60 *Minutes* that Omar would return to "take his revenge."[18]

This is the home Omar Khadr will be returning to: one where his mother, Maha, said her reaction to watching the planes crash into the World Trade Center towers on 9/11 was "let them have it," who doesn't believe suicide bombing is wrong, and who says she's proud of Omar for killing Sergeant Speer.[19] One where his brother, Abdullah Khadr, is facing charges for procuring weapons for al Qaeda.[20] And one where his sister Zaynab, on the day the United States announced it had killed Osama bin Laden, posted a portrait of the terrorist kingpin on her Facebook page, announcing that the Muslim world would "be in mourning for 3 days . . . may [A]llah give us the saber and strength to keep up the fight . . . Ameen."[21] While in Guantanamo, Khadr's own devotion to his perverted interpretation of Islam has only intensified: we know he has memorized the Koran while in custody, and that he now leads his cell block in daily prayers. Even Khadr's own lawyer, Dennis Edney, has publicly conceded that his client should be de-radicalized when he returns to Canada[22]; in all his time at Guantanamo, Khadr hasn't been exposed to any efforts to moderate his deadly beliefs. Can any reasonable person expect that, once in Canada – back among his al Qaeda family after spending nearly a decade being jailed by infidel Americans, plotting to "take his revenge" – Omar Khadr will be any more rehabilitated than the 150 terrorists who returned to their fight after walking out of Guantanamo Bay?

CHAPTER 12

KHADR'S HOMECOMING

"Khadr voluntarily chose to conspire and agree with various members of al Qaeda to train and ultimately conduct operations to kill United States and coalition forces. Khadr's efforts in attending, training, constructing and planting IEDs, and ultimately participating in a fire-fight against U.S. forces, were all in support of al Qaeda and furthered the aims of the terrorist group."

Confession of Omar Ahmed Khadr, October 13, 2010

So, what can we expect to happen with Omar Khadr when he inevitably returns to Canada?

Unfortunately, it's not hard to guess. When Maher Arar came back to Canada after he was released from a prison in Syria, he was hailed as a hero and celebrity. Every anti-war, anti-Western activist with an axe to grind – which includes a large swath of Canada's mainstream media – turned his homecoming into a triumph. If only they treated our wounded soldiers returning from Afghanistan so warmly.

Maher Arar was arrested by America too, in September 2002. But it wasn't on a battlefield, caught throwing live grenades and shooting at translators and medics. The Syrian-born Ottawa resident was arrested at JFK International Airport in New York on his way back to Canada after spending time in Tunisia.[1] Washington suspected him of having links to al Qaeda and deported him to Syria. Canada's Liberal government, harbouring its own suspicions of Arar, did not protest. Arar confessed to his Syrian interrogators that he had trained with the Mujahideen in Afghanistan in 1993 but later recanted, insisting he falsely confessed under serious physical torture. He was whipped with cables, he said, though no medical evidence of that torture has ever been produced – despite a sweeping federal commission set up to review the Arar case – and when the Department of Foreign Affairs once asked Arar's family to provide evidence of his whereabouts during the period in question, they did not.[2] Omar Khadr actually identified Arar as someone he'd seen at an al Qaeda safe house in Afghanistan,[3] according to the sworn testimony of an FBI agent who interrogated Khadr.

Nonetheless, Maher Arar sued the Canadian government in 2004, alleging negligence, negligent investigation, defamation, false imprisonment, assault and battery, and abuse of public office, claiming Canadian security officials fingered him for scrutiny "on the basis of racial and cultural stereotypes and prejudices."[4] The government settled in 2007, handing Arar an apology along with a $10.5 million payout, and another $1 million to cover his legal bills.[5]

Not surprisingly, Nate Whitling, Omar Khadr's co-counsel along with Dennis Edney, filed a lawsuit in 2010 against the Canadian government seeking $10 million in damages for allowing his client to remain in U.S. custody these past years.[6] The fact that Khadr has admitted to being a terrorist, a murderer, and a spy can't have dampened Whitling's enthusiasm one bit. And with the multi-million-dollar precedent set by Arar, what lawyer wouldn't be excited about a lawsuit like this one?

But trying to squeeze millions of dollars out of Canada's taxpayers – for having the gall to not stop the Americans from detaining him and trying him for war crimes to which he would eventually confess – would just be the first order of business for the celebrity darling of the Canadian left. Like Maher Arar, Khadr is destined to become a political poster boy for the anti-American, terror-apologist wing. Arar's wife, Monia Mazigh, actually ran for a seat in the federal government in 2004, riding the wave of sympathy for her husband, and the New Democratic Party (NDP) considered her their "star candidate" because of it.[7] As a Muslim, Mazigh opposed many of the NDP's traditional policies on issues like gay rights and abortion.[8] But the sole fact that she was married to a living icon for the anti-War-on-Terror propaganda effort was more than enough for Canada's left-wingers to forgive her decidedly unprogressive views on those other subjects (Ottawa's voters were less enamoured with her, though; Mazigh lost the race).

Maher Arar meantime, flush with a taxpayer-funded settlement, has launched an online magazine[9] offering "in-depth coverage and analysis of national security related issues," which includes articles denouncing Canada's extradition laws[10] and accusing Canada of "complicity" with torture,[11] while his own website invites journalists to call for media interviews through his agent (who also publishes the magazine).[12] While Arar was busy working up his media exposure, his wife, Mazigh, further expanded the Arar publicity machine when she published in 2007 a book about her husband's year-long imprisonment. In it, she writes: "I have seen myself change status from victim and wife of a presumed terrorist to modern-day heroine of the likes of even Laura Secord."[13]

Khadr doesn't have a wife to run as a "star candidate" for the NDP or to write a 272-page declaration of her love and his innocence. But he's a star in his own right – a terrorist who had a personal relationship with Osama bin Laden; who fought and killed Americans in Afghanistan; who made both the U.S. and Canadian governments blink; and who will likely be back on the streets, a free man, still in his twenties.

If Maher Arar became a minor celebrity after his wrangle with the Syrian security system, with a secondary role played by Washington and Ottawa, it's a virtual lock that Omar Khadr – the leading man in a supposed morality play pitting the Bush administration, perennial bugbear of the left, and its Guantanamo "gulag" against a purportedly naive and pitiable "child soldier" from Canada – is set to become nothing less than a superstar.

Unlike Arar, who enjoyed only a fraction of the sympathy and media coverage, Khadr will be coming home to the built-in fan club that he's amassed since his capture. Arlette Zinck, the professor at Edmonton's King's University College who struck up a tender pen pal relationship with Khadr – "Whenever you are lonesome, remember you have many friends who keep you in their prayers. Each morning at 9 o'clock, I include you in mine," she wrote to him in Guantanamo, referring to Khadr as "my dear student"[14] – has led the charge in turning her campus into a factory for Khadr groupies. Zinck actually testified in Khadr's defence, calling him a "considerate young man . . . thoughtful and generous in spirit"[15] in a sentencing hearing for a murder he himself confessed he took pleasure in reminiscing about (how considerate). In 2008, her school hosted a talk by Dennis Edney, one of Khadr's lawyers, to give a speech about how "a young Muslim man has been branded a terrorist without trial" and the failures of the Canadian government in supporting Khadr's case.[16] Along with a "consortium of activist groups,"[17] Zinck's students organized a rally later that year drawing seven hundred Khadr supporters to cheer for Khadr in downtown Edmonton,[18] and Zinck herself has said she would personally recommend Omar Khadr's application to attend King's University College as a mature student.[19]

But then he probably won't have the time. Or the need. Omar Khadr isn't likely to spend much time in prison once he applies to be released to Canadian custody in late 2011 after serving just one additional year in Gitmo (part of the plea agreement with the Obama administration). Under current Canadian law, Khadr should be able to apply for parole after serving one-third of his sentence – and his nine years in pre-trial custody means he's already done that (even statutory release kicks in after two-thirds of a sentence).[20] A free man, he'll have a career waiting for him here in Canada as a top speaker on the anti-American lecture circuit. Every pro-Islamist campus club, every unreformed mosque, as well as conferences for the reflexively anti-American New Democratic Party and the Canadian Bar Association, the national lawyers' group that for years churned out reams of press releases calling for Khadr's release and return to Canada, all are sure to hound the freed terrorist to come speak to them, paying him thousands of dollars an hour for the pleasure.

The Canadian Islamic Congress and Canadian Arab Federation have been vocal supporters of Khadr's defence[21,22] and will surely welcome him with open arms onto their staff: who better to fundraise among their Israel-hating, America-hating supporters? Perhaps Judy Rebick – the founding publisher of the left-wing webzine Rabble.ca, who hailed Khadr as a new Nelson Mandela – will offer him a regular column to share his views with thousands of readers, and, as a professor of social justice and democracy at Toronto's Ryerson University,[23] maybe she'll make him a featured speaker at her school. That is, when he isn't busy with Professor Zinck's students. No doubt both will be in a race with hard-left universities like York University in Toronto, the University of Ottawa, and Concordia University in Montreal to be the first to award Omar Khadr an honorary doctorate degree. He could be the first terrorist ever nominated for the Order of Canada. What's less sure is that the nomination will be declined.

Khadr will be courted by on-campus radio stations and left-wing reporters, becoming the go-to guy to comment on radical Islam, terrorism, Afghanistan, the fight against al Qaeda, American security, the evils of Israel, and a hundred other topics where his supposed expertise can be deployed to advance the same distorted worldview that's been used to tilt virtually every Khadr story reported here over the last nine years.

If the CBC isn't already planning a reality show around Omar Khadr and what they'd surely call his "struggles" to adapt back into Canadian society, it's because they're not quite quick enough on the uptake: just give them a few more months and tax dollars. Khadr's plea deal with the U.S. government may forbid him from personally profiting from telling stories about his crimes or the time he spent in Guantanamo Bay, but even if that portion of his plea deal with Washington were enforceable in Canada, it would be stunningly simple to get around: either by funnelling the money to someone else – perhaps even another fellow jihadi – or by ensuring that whenever and wherever he speaks, he refers to it as a more general discussion about the evils of Islamophobia.

Other notorious murderers have to live under strict conditions when they're released: the child-killer Karla Homolka was ordered to keep police constantly apprised of her whereabouts after she was let out of prison.[24] But will Canada's National Parole Board require anything like that for Khadr? And as he's travelling the country for all his speaking tours, media appearances, and awards, how many Canadians will be forced to share an airplane ride with the committed al Qaeda terrorist? There's nothing right now that would stop the avowed jihadi from boarding the same Air Canada flight as you and your family, nor from loitering outside synagogues and Hebrew schools. What fun it will be for Canadians to have to live with a confessed murdering Islamist walking free among them (you can be sure that any attempts by police or security to keep tabs on Khadr will be met with vigorous civil rights lawsuits by his friends in the Canadian Bar Association, and any landlord who refuses to rent him a flat or employer who refuses him a job is bound to find him- or herself in court facing down a phalanx of pro-Khadr lawyers).

The spectacle of an admitted al Qaeda terrorist with American blood on his hands smiling down at us from podiums and TV screens for years to come is chilling enough. But what's sure to prove even more alarming about all the publicity and support that Omar Khadr is bound to enjoy when he comes home is that there's nothing to stop him from spewing whatever vileness he wants. No one can tell Omar Khadr what to say. He can condemn our American allies – or our own soldiers – before a national audience with all the vitriol of a radical imam and get paid handsomely for it; he can denounce Canada and our soldiers just as easily. And, yes, he's perfectly free to share his vicious hatred for Jews, Christians, and Americans. Omar Khadr will be free to spout as many militant lies as he likes, and, unlike other dangerous Islamists and al Qaeda supporters, he's got a massive and sympathetic national fan base eager to hear him out.

After all, other terrorists released from Guantanamo Bay are frequently compelled to complete at least some kind of nominal de-radicalization process before being released again onto the streets of their home countries.[25] But there's nothing to date requiring Omar Khadr to do any such thing. Even German soldiers, after the Second World War, were required by the Allies to complete "deNazification" programs to rehabilitate their odious views about Jews and other minorities.[26] After years of stewing in the propaganda and hatred of Hitler's suffocating culture of indoctrination, they required some sort of antidote. Khadr, meanwhile, went from growing up with a family of terrorist radicals to palling around with terrorist radicals in the Hindu Kush, to spending his days consorting and studying the Koran with terrorist radicals in Guantanamo Bay. Don't expect him to return to Canada as a big supporter of multi-ethnic harmony, democracy, women's rights, and peace.

Even one of his own lawyers, Dennis Edney, admits that Khadr needs to be de-radicalized and has suggested a plan to do it. There are just a few problems with his proposal. For one thing, one of the Muslim leaders who stood alongside Dennis Edney at the February 2009 press conference announcing this planned rehabilitation was a man named Zafar Bangash, the president of the Islamic Society of York Region, in Toronto. "We have a plan in place," Bangash said, that would involve "close supervision," and Khadr "would be provided spiritual counseling."[27]

But Bangash may not be quite the right guy to be rehabilitating someone away from the more poisonous strains of radical Islam. A supporter of Ayatollah Khomeini, Bangash has accused U.S. president Barack Obama of being a "slave" of the American establishment and has said his presidency promotes "American and Zionist crimes"; he has called Israelis "thugs"[28] and "thieves and bandits from Europe and America" who should go "back where they came from."[29] He's said Washington enabled the 9/11 attacks. "Perhaps . . . part of the U.S. establishment wanted this to happen because they had perhaps another agenda to pursue," he said. He's declared himself and his fans "in favour of the Islamic revolution in Iran." In the *Crescent International*, the pro-Iranian newspaper he founded, Westerners are labelled "murderous, racist and virulent" and Canada a "paid-up member of the Anglo-Saxon mafia, which is responsible for most of the recorded genocides in the world."[30] He believes Israel was secretly behind the attempted Christmas Day underwear bombing on Northwest Airlines flight 253 in 2009.[31]

In one edition of his newspaper, Bangash gave an entire page over to Hamas, the Palestinian terrorist group that is sworn to the murder of Jews.[32] "Sons of Islam everywhere, jihad is an obligation upon you, to establish the Rule of Allah on Earth, and to liberate your lands and yourselves from the hegemony of America and its Zionist allies," wrote the then-leader of Hamas Sheikh Ahmad Yaseen on Bangash's pages.

Putting Omar Khadr through a "de-radicalization" program like that definitely won't make Canadians feel any safer about having the prince of al Qaeda walking their streets.

There's a second problem with Edney's proposal for a "de-radicalization plan" as well. That is: Omar Khadr probably can't be rehabilitated. Certainly not under the current circumstances.

That's the conclusion of forensic psychiatric expert Dr. Michael Welner. Based on his research into Islamic terrorists and which factors contribute to their likelihood of returning to terrorism once they're released from prison, Dr. Welner determined that the main factors informing the likelihood of rehabilitation are (1) whether the terrorist feels remorse for his actions and (2) the level of "Westernization" of the terrorist.[33]

Dr. Welner conducted two days of interviews one-on-one with Omar Khadr; interviewed officials (guards, medical personnel) who had direct contact with Khadr; and reviewed dozens of tapes, transcripts, and records documenting virtually everything Khadr did and said since he was taken into U.S. custody. And based on all of this, he came away with a very sobering conclusion: Omar Khadr has never shown remorse for his actions.

Careful observers of the Khadr trial likely sensed this already, even through the thick fog of biased reporting surrounding Guantanamo. When Khadr testified at his own trial, he might have tried to at least act partly contrite, but it definitely didn't come out that way. Speaking to Christopher Speer's widow, Tabitha, he said: "I'm really, really sorry for the pain I caused your family."[34] Notice he didn't say he was sorry for what he did, for killing another human being, or becoming a terrorist. The best he could manage was to try to sound sympathetic to a woman and two children who weren't present that day in Khost and yet suffered as much as anyone. It was the kind of weasely apology that you often hear from slick politicians caught in some kind of scandal – expressing their regret that something happened, instead of simply saying they did something wrong. Omar Khadr wasn't sorry for being a terrorist; he was merely acknowledging that terrorism, necessary as he believes it is, comes with certain costs. "I'm really, really sorry for the pain I've caused your family," Khadr said. "I wish I could do something to take this pain away from you. That's really all I can say."[35]

Dr. Welner noticed the same pattern when he studied and interviewed Khadr. He "regretted having done something that would cause him to be brought here to GTMO," he testified at Khadr's sentencing hearing.[36] Khadr's remorse, as it were, "was primarily related to his being in custody, having been brought to custody, as opposed to killing Christopher Speer and having laid mines that had substantial destructive potential," said Dr. Welner. When Dr. Welner confronted Khadr with evidence of his terrorist activity, such as the videotape of Khadr building bombs, Khadr didn't show remorse then either. He was, Dr. Welner testified, "resentful at having to be confronted with his actions and annoyed at the whole experience." Dr. Welner finally asked Khadr outright if he regretted any of his actions. Khadr's response was "defensiveness . . . he essentially said that he had nothing to regret."[37]

"I actually think the anti-anti-terror sector created Omar Khadr" as he is today, Dr. Welner said in an interview. "He would have people going down and cheerleading him, and they enabled him then, and they enable him now, and they'll enable him when he gets out." Assuring him that he had nothing to be sorry for, that what he did was beyond his control and not his fault, Dr. Welner says, "disincentivized him from being accountable." In the interview, the tape of which the defence fought tooth and nail to keep out of the trial, "he comes across as spoiled and immature, somebody who's used to being pampered, who never had to be accountable," he says. That's what the defence team didn't want the jury to see. "To watch him is to appreciate what an entitled young man he is. He just doesn't get it." He doesn't believe he belongs in prison because so many people have assured him of it, Dr. Welner says. How can Khadr be remorseful when he's been repeatedly told he has done nothing wrong and that his incarceration is unjust? "I don't entirely blame him for this," Dr. Welner says. "I think by the time he came to me, he had been indoctrinated by his anti-Gitmo amen corner."

Still, you might think that someone like Omar Khadr, raised in Scarborough, Harry Potter fan, fluent in English, would score high on the "Westernization" dimension that is so critical to a terrorist's rehabilitation. But you'd be wrong. Dr. Welner noted in his testimony that in Khadr's significant time spent away from Canada, he has become increasingly non-Westernized. In Guantanamo, he chose to memorize the entire Koran and now leads a cell block "composed of entirely devout confederates" in prayers.[38] There are more than six thousand verses in the Koran in 114 chapters, or *suras*. Memorizing it requires an immense amount of patience and determination. Not to mention religious fervour. And while Khadr was happy to devote himself to it, Dr. Welner noticed that, aside from some language classes, Khadr had done almost no studying of anything else. He was given all manner of books and materials to teach him the Canadian curriculum beyond the Grade 8 education he was given by his parents. But "he took no initiative to develop himself academically in secular studies," Dr. Welner observed. "So he's the one who leads [prayers] because the others have that level of regard for him reflecting his study and skill, and yet, he has not invested anywhere near a comparable energy in developing himself academically."[39]

As far as Khadr's acculturation with Western values goes, Dr. Welner said there is simply "no evidence" of it. Quite the opposite. "He reads Harry Potter but, you know, in terms of reading escapist materials, which is what he has actually described to me, he reads things just to get away, to not think about things. He is very angry about being in custody, but he does not involve himself in the kinds of things that would acculturate him to this western environment."[40]

As Dr. Welner pointed out on the stand, a poor prognosis for recidivism, violence, and poor reintegration comes with being religiously devout, which Omar Khadr has indisputably been ever since his capture – arguably more so than before he was caught. The more devout one is, the more likely one is to be submissive to the Koran, since the word *Islam* itself means "submission." And when an individual believes that the Koran tells him or her that it is justified to kill Jews and infidels and that martyrdom will be rewarded in the afterlife with seventy-two virgins, that religiosity can only lead that person back again to terror.

A poor prognosis also comes with being angry and bitter, something Khadr repeatedly proved he remains. "He's full of rage," Dr. Welner determined. "It is his belief that he shouldn't have been here for a day, that he shouldn't have been here for a minute, and that it is everybody else's fault that he is here." And a poor prognosis, Dr. Welner's research shows, also has to do with who the terrorist identifies with. Khadr has been "in a radical jihadist community . . . the people that he is around are thoroughly devoted to that ideology; they are bitter and belligerent enemies of the United States," Dr. Welner testified. De-radicalization, in the rare occasions that it's successful, requires changing a terrorist's deviant thinking; it requires a cleric, well versed in the Koran, to convince a terrorist that the violent, murderous interpretation of the holy book is wrong, and to make a compelling case that it does not justify terrorism or command intolerance.[41]

What Dr. Welner observed in Khadr is that he doesn't recognize any religious influences besides himself; "he's his own influence."[42] And so, as it stands, Khadr's interpretation of the Koran – the one that justified his murder of Christopher Speer, the one that he believes entitled him to plant bombs, the one that he believes entitled him to plunder the money of the infidels – remains the interpretation he continues to operate from. He has learned no other way. Dr. Welner testified, "This individual is a man who keeps his own counsel. He's fired attorneys. He makes his own mind up. He goes to his own tune. He is his own spiritual guide. Who has the power to penetrate that?"[43]

Finally, Khadr's primary influence outside of Guantanamo remains, of course, his own terrorist crime family. In the minority of cases where de-radicalization programs do succeed, it's with men who have yet to commit terrorist acts, or have committed very minor ones,[44] and it's almost always at the request of worried family members alarmed at the dark turn their loved one's religious path has taken. The family, then, takes "ownership of responsibility to make sure that when he's no longer in [the] program, that he stays deradicalized."[45] De-radicalization, Dr. Welner noted, is not a "revolving door," and it's not a sure fix: there are men who have graduated successfully from Singapore's de-radicalization program, and there are men who may be there their whole lives because they are not safe to release to the community and may never be. Omar Khadr has never taken responsibility for his terrorism, he's angry he had to pay for it, he believes his radical version of the Koran is the correct one and is more committed to it than ever, and his only support network back home in Toronto is a family that remains proud of his terrorism – his mother calls him "our little hero"[46] – and committed to the cause of al Qaeda.

Dr. Welner says he absolutely believes that de-radicalization is necessary for violent jihadists before they can be safely released from detainment. And he believes that Khadr certainly needs it before he can be considered safe to release to Canada. But above all he believes that there is little chance Khadr will get the proper de-radicalization program he needs (there are no such formal programs in Canada) and that even if one were forced upon him, it would, given his lack of remorse, his anger and bitterness toward Americans and Canadians, and his increased devotion to his family's radical version of Islam, almost certainly fail. "Omar Khadr is a high risk of dangerousness as a radical jihadist," Dr. Welner told the court.[47]

But even if somehow there was a faint hope of the imam from York Region actually having some slight positive influence on Khadr, there's one more problem with lawyer Dennis Edney's homemade de-radicalization plan: Omar Khadr wouldn't have to follow it. Edney may think it sounds like a smart public relations move to attempt some rehabilitation program – he even realizes it's actually necessary given that Khadr's spent his entire life believing in hate and violence. But even if this were a more legitimate de-radicalization process being proposed, the government couldn't order Omar Khadr to take it. If he is released from prison at the end of his sentence for time served, Khadr would be a free man: free to leverage all the sympathy he's amassed in his years in prison for murder to spread whatever perverted ideas he wants – all the while forcing Canadians to tolerate him walking their streets, flying in their airplanes, and lecturing them about his views on America, Jews, the Middle East, and anything else he chooses, from their television sets.

But enough public outrage could cause Canada's legal system to grudgingly keep Khadr behind bars. If Canadian courts don't give him credit for time served, and if he's treated as an adult, not a young offender, Khadr could serve as much as two and a half years in jail before being paroled. And the parole board could put conditions on him, such as living in a halfway house and seeking employment. Section 810.01 of the Criminal Code allows a judge to order participation in a treatment program or even the wearing of a monitoring device.

It's theoretically possible – it could happen that Canada's legal establishment will suddenly make a 180-degree change in their view of Khadr, and treat him as a convicted terrorist. Even then, he'll be out on our streets while still in his twenties. But there's only one sure way: convincing the Conservative government not to let him back into Canada in the first place.

The Khadrs were once upon a time considered among the most reviled, most dangerous people ever to make this country their home. Thanks to years of hard cheerleading on our campuses, in our political movements, and in our newsrooms for the family's most favoured son, Canada will soon become Omar Khadr's country. The rest of us will just be forced to live in it.

CHAPTER 13

BLOCK KHADR'S·RETURN

I have taken into account that other U.S. federal govern-
ment agencies have indicated their willingness to positively
endorse my prisoner transfer application after I have
completed one additional year in U.S. custody after my
sentence is approved: however, I recognize the decision to
approve my transfer is ultimately made by the Canadian
Government and this agreement cannot bind Canadian
Officials to accept my prisoner transfer application.

Omar Khadr's pre-trial plea offer, October 13, 2010

In his 2008 presidential campaign, Barack Obama repeatedly promised to shut down the U.S. prison for terrorists at Guantanamo Bay, Cuba. After becoming president, he didn't: the heavy responsibilities of a president leading a War on Terror quickly replaced the easy promises of an inexperienced candidate. But getting rid of Guantanamo's celebrity inmate, Omar Khadr, remained a political priority.

And so, despite conclusive evidence of Khadr's crimes – including video footage of Khadr assembling terrorist bombs – the Obama administration offered Khadr a plea bargain. He would be sentenced to eight years for his terrorist crimes but need serve only a single year in a U.S. prison. After that, he could be returned to Canada, where he would be eligible for full parole immediately. That deal was accepted by Khadr on October 13, 2010, but its terms were kept secret from the U.S. jury at Guantanamo Bay that still met to sentence Khadr. They handed him a forty-year sentence.

Forty years, pled down to one year. That's a 97.5 per cent discount.

But the deal wasn't just between Obama's prosecutors and Khadr. Canada played an essential part in issuing the get-out-of-jail-free card. Without Canada's diplomatic assurances, the promise of a transfer back to Canada – and to freedom – would have been meaningless. Without Ottawa's nod at allowing a confessed and convicted al Qaeda terrorist back on to Canadian soil, Khadr wouldn't have accepted the plea and Obama's prosecutors wouldn't have offered it. In fact, the deal specifically promised that the Canadian Department of Foreign Affairs would give Khadr a "diplomatic note" confirming their support for the plea deal.

So Canada's Conservative government, which had for years so vigorously fought off court challenges to compel them to bring Khadr back to Canada, battling a full court press of public attacks from Khadr's personal lobby in the media, the legal profession, and opportunist politicians throughout, suddenly gave everything away in a fire sale.

It's one thing for a liberal U.S. Democrat to go soft on crime. But what about Stephen Harper's Conservatives, who have made criminal justice, including "truth in sentencing," a centrepiece of their political platform? The Conservatives are planning to build more prisons in Canada, to eliminate extra credit for time served in custody awaiting trial, to toughen up penalties for drug- and firearm-related crimes, and to limit the discretion a judge can exercise in sentencing criminals for a number of felonies by legislating absolute minimum sentences.

The Conservatives aren't only tough on crime; they've been tough on terrorism too. Canadian prosecutors sought – and received – harsh penalties for homegrown terrorists, such as the Toronto 18, who plotted to attack Canadian buildings including the CN Tower and Parliament Hill. Zakaria Amara, just a year or so older than Omar Khadr, received a life sentence from a Canadian court for his plot to blow up buildings in downtown Toronto.[1] Like Khadr, he had planned for mass murder; unlike Khadr, he didn't actually get the opportunity to spill any blood.

Terrorists on the street in Canada are taken seriously. And terrorism in Afghanistan isn't an abstract matter for Canadians either; more than 150 Canadian Forces personnel have died there, the overwhelming majority of them brutally killed by improvised explosive devices exactly like the ones Khadr was filmed assembling. In fact, the very first Canadian casualty in Afghanistan fell victim to an IED planted by a teenager.

Yet Khadr's sweetheart deal was approved by the Canadian Conservative government in a series of secret negotiations. The Canadian public was kept in the dark until the deal was already done. U.S. prosecutors were bushwhacked. The agreement was signed by Khadr, his two lawyers, and two representatives of the U.S. government, but it was cooked up in a backroom deal among Obama's inner circle, Khadr's lawyers, and a cooperative Canadian government. Khadr's one-year U.S. sentence is set to expire in October 2011, and his transfer to Canada could happen any time after that.

Khadr wants that to happen. So does the Obama administration. And so do a lot of Khadr's allies, from the

Canadian Bar Association to the CBC. And, of course, no one wants Khadr's public release more than al Qaeda itself, who knows the immense public relations value that comes with having a convicted terrorist set free, triumphant and remorseless. Khadr has never abandoned his grotesque, murderous interpretation of the Koran and Islam; he has never once renounced his allegiance to al Qaeda; and throughout his detention, his family, a pillar of the al Qaeda community, has continued to propagandize for Islamism and to publicly undermine the Canadian and American war against terror. His release is an advertisement for al Qaeda, both in revealing the weakness of will it has always accused Westerners of possessing and in recruiting yet more teenagers to its cause by proving that they, like Khadr, will escape harsh punishment should they ever be caught murdering Western soldiers.

But there is a way to stop it. Two ways, actually. And there is just enough time.

The plea bargain sets out the deal between Obama and Khadr. It promises that Khadr can return to Canada after one year. But the second-last paragraph of the seven-page deal has this important note in it: the U.S. government does not have the authority to "bind the government of Canada to allow the accused to enter the country, or to direct, control or otherwise influence the accused's confinement, transfer, parole, or release while in the custody of the government of Canada."[2]

The United States promises to do all the paperwork necessary to transfer Khadr. But they say very clearly.

that they can't force Canada to comply with the deal.

The secret Canadian "diplomatic notes" to Khadr, confirming Ottawa's support for Obama's plea bargain, have never been publicly revealed. We don't know what, exactly, was in them, but they were obviously persuasive enough to make Khadr accept the bargain – and persuasive enough to permit the U.S. government to offer the bargain to Khadr in the first place. "Canada's language is sufficiently satisfactory to uphold Canada to its position that it will take Omar Khadr back after one year. And the American language is even stronger," Khadr's Canadian lawyer, Dennis Edney, said, about the diplomatic notes.[3] But according to Canadian law, promises from Canadian diplomats, even promises from Canada's foreign minister, are not sufficient to allow a convicted terrorist to be imported from a U.S. jail onto Canadian streets. There are two legal barriers – two lines of defence that could stop the Obama administration from freeing the prince of al Qaeda and shipping him to Canada.

The first is a Canadian law called the International Transfer of Offenders Act (ITOA). Section 10 of the ITOA states that the decision to accept a prisoner from another country is made not by the foreign minister but by the minister of public safety – at the time of writing, this was Vic Toews.

And whereas Canada's diplomats may have had political reasons to agree to the transfer – pleasing President Obama, making nice with a powerful ally and trading partner, or perhaps indulging their own personal politics on the War on Terror – the factors Toews must consider, according to the ITOA, are outlined in some detail. And pleasing the U.S. president isn't on the list.

Section 10(1)(a) of the ITOA, for example, states that Canada must consider whether the transfer of Khadr "would constitute a threat to the security of Canada." That should be the beginning and end of the decision process right there. Khadr is a remorseless, cold-blooded killer who has become only more hardened in prison and whose own lawyer has conceded requires "de-radicalization," while an expert forensic psychiatrist testified that such a process was almost certainly hopeless for Khadr and that he remained "highly dangerous" and therefore plainly represents a clear and present threat to Canadian security. But there are three other considerations that the law requires – each of which leans against Khadr.

Section 10(1)(b) of the law asks whether Khadr "left or remained outside Canada with the intention of abandoning Canada as [his] place of permanent residence." That's clearly another instrument in Toews's toolbox that he could and, according to the ITOA, must use in order to keep Omar Khadr from returning to Canada. Of course Khadr left this country with the intention of abandoning it as his home. His spent nearly his entire life in Pakistan and Afghanistan. Instead of trying to return to Canada, he chose to join al Qaeda and fight in Afghanistan until he became a martyr. He had no more attachment to Canada than the rest of his family, viewing us as a source of free health care, fundraising for terrorism, and a convenient, if temporary, safe haven for whenever things got bad.

Section 10(1)(c) asks whether Khadr has "social or family ties" in Canada. But the only real ties he has here – not counting the journalists and left-wing activists who have never actually met him and so can't possibly be considered tied to him – are to his family members. Most of whom are a self-described cell of al Qaeda.

The final legal criterion in Canada's International Transfer of Offenders Act asks whether the foreign jail that Khadr is in "presents a serious threat to the offender's security or human rights." That's a provision to bring back Canadian criminals from jails run by barbaric regimes like Iran or North Korea, where prisoners are routinely tortured or starved. As we all know, Guantanamo Bay is more pleasant than any Canadian prison would be, with everything from big-screen TVs to video games to lots of sports – and all of it constantly under strict scrutiny by America's lawyers and courts. Khadr's stay there has been more comfortable than what he would have experienced here, what with all those special goodies and creature comforts constantly being delivered to him. Khadr himself admitted that his life was so pleasant at Gitmo, he wouldn't mind terribly if he stayed there. Clearly, there is nothing about Khadr's stay in Guantanamo that presents any threat to his human rights.

The ITOA was amended in 2004, in the aftermath of 9/11. And so section 10(2) adds one more level of scrutiny with respect to criminals wanting to come home to

Canada, namely, "whether, in the Minister's opinion, the offender will, after the transfer, commit a terrorism offence or criminal organization offence."

How likely is Khadr to commit more terrorist acts or other crimes? It's up to Toews and his department – including CSIS and the RCMP – to make that very serious assessment. Not politicians, diplomats, bureaucrats, or lawyers.

Dr. Michael Welner's forensic psychiatric report shows that Khadr has all of the hallmarks of a terrorist who will commit more crimes. Even during his sentencing hearing, when he took the stand briefly, Khadr refused to express regret for his jihad, saying only that he regretted the pain suffered by Sergeant Speer's widow – not the murder that caused the pain.

Dr. Welner's testimony was powerful, powerful enough that, after jurors heard it, their verdict was to keep Khadr in prison until he was sixty-four. But unbeknownst to them, it was secretly pre-empted by the Obama administration's plea deal, which could see Khadr out on Canada's streets as early as this year.

Who will Toews listen to? To President Obama, who wants to rid himself of the problem of Omar Khadr, to offload him here in Canada, where he becomes our problem instead of a problem for the U.S. military that originally charged and prosecuted him? To Canadian diplomats, who want to curry favour at the White House? Or to the gruesome confession of the unreformed terrorist himself, whose own lawyer says he has not been de-radicalized?

Toews has a reputation as a law-and-order politician – a reputation he built in his former capacity as justice minister for Manitoba and again in that role in Stephen Harper's first government. His natural instincts would surely be to apply the ITOA to the facts of one of the most dangerous terrorists in Guantanamo Bay – and to keep Khadr out of this country, and off of our streets, for as long as possible. But will Toews's instincts be enough to override pressure from Canada's Department of Foreign Affairs, backed up by the CBC, the *Toronto Star*, the Canadian Bar Association, and every terrorist apologist in the country? Barack Obama didn't even have to deal with the continual assault by the "Guantanamo's Child" lobby, and still he somehow went soft on Khadr. It would be nice to believe that Toews is made of much sterner stuff – and he'd have to be – but there's no guarantee of it.

If Toews caves in to that pressure, there is still one more line of defence: the National Parole Board (NPB).

The NPB, which decides whether to release prisoners from jail before they finish their full sentence, is notoriously lax. Full parole is routinely granted for violent criminals after they complete just one-third of their sentence. For others, so-called statutory release frees all but the most dangerous criminals after they have served just two-thirds of their sentence. But on those rare occasions when the glare of public scrutiny is on them, the NPB has declined to give lenient parole. The case of Clifford Olson, who murdered eleven children, is one example. Seventy years old, he was denied parole in 2010 for the second time in four years, almost certainly because of the public outrage that would have erupted were that monster ever to be let loose. Even Olson knew it. "I know I'm going to be turned down," he said before the hearing, and afterward he said he wouldn't even bother applying again.[4]

Both Toews and the NPB are required by statute to consider the risks to the public of releasing Khadr from prison early. And here is the key to stopping them from doing so, and to providing John Baird, appointed Canada's foreign minister in 2011, with a political excuse for reneging on the diplomatic deal made with the White House.

The true nature of Khadr's dangerousness was kept a secret from the Canadian government when the Obama administration was pressuring it to accept their plea deal. In fact, the most gruesome evidence about Khadr's mind is still being kept from Canadian authorities.

The plea deal was struck in the days before October 13, 2010. But the testimony of Dr. Michael Welner, the forensic psychiatrist who interviewed Khadr at length, had not yet been given at his trial in Guantanamo Bay. His psychiatric report had not yet been made public. Dr. Welner – the top FBI expert, the psychiatrist who developed the "Depravity Scale" to codify the heinousness of crimes – hadn't yet given his opinion about the depth of Khadr's evil. He had not yet testified that he considered Khadr to be "highly dangerous" in terms of his risk to return to terror.

But none of that was known to the Canadian government, or the Canadian public, when the deal was cooked up. Nor have they seen those videotapes of Dr. Welner's actual jailhouse interviews with Khadr, the ones that Khadr's defence lawyers were so desparate to keep from being allowed into evidence. The Obama administration knew about those videotapes and Dr. Welner's report all along – it was U.S. prosecutors who hired Dr. Welner to assess Khadr. Partly on the basis of Dr. Welner's assessment, the jury sentenced Khadr to forty years in prison. Yet to this day, Dr. Welner's eight hours of video interviews with Khadr are kept secret, under seal in the Guantanamo Bay court. They have not been shown to the Canadian government, let alone released to the Canadian public – the very people who will soon be told they must accept Khadr back on their streets.

What is in those videotapes that Khadr's defence lawyers fought so intensely to keep from being tabled as evidence in his trial? Why can't Toews see them? Why can't the National Parole Board see them? Are they not relevant to the key consideration of whether Khadr should be allowed back into the country? Are they not key to the consideration of public safety?

How could either Toews or the NPB approve Khadr for public release without all the facts in front of them? How could they even attempt to consider the matter, knowing that they are being kept in the dark by the American government?

Foreign Minister Baird must demand a copy of the Khadr tapes for Public Safety Minister Toews to review before he conducts the review described by the prisoner transfer law. It's outrageous enough that the White House kept those tapes from Canada while pressing our diplomats to agree to the plea deal; it's unacceptable that they suppress that damning information required for the ITOA to be properly implemented.

If the United States backs down and hands over the videos to Toews, he must not do to us what the Americans have done to him. He must release the video to the Canadian public before rendering his opinion. If he doesn't, it would just be a replay of the secret negotiations that lead to the plea deal – an admission that the facts are too damning for mere citizens to see.

If Toews approves the transfer – which would be going against everything he's said in a lifetime of law enforcement and the Conservatives' promises about crime control, truth in sentencing, and respecting our troops and our allies' troops – then the National Parole Board must hold an open hearing in which those eight hours of interview videos are laid bare for the public to see. Sgt. Christopher Speer's widow must be invited to testify. And so must Sgt. Layne Morris, the soldier partially blinded for life by Omar Khadr and his al Qaeda gang.

It's clear why Obama wants to rid himself of Omar Khadr – it's a political bone for him to throw to the antiwar left in compensation for keeping Guantanamo Bay open. And however foolish an American president's request of us may be, our country's prime minister, given the special relationship between Canada and the United States, would be wise not to refuse lightly.

But a request for the transfer of a confessed and committed murderer and terrorist is not a normal request. This is not about an obscure trade regulation or some financial squabble. It's a brazen demand for Canada to put a confessed murderer on Canadian streets so that the U.S. president can save face with his anti-war base. That's not statecraft or serious international relations. It's using Canadian streets as a garbage dump.

The secrecy of the negotiations between the White House and the Canadian government proves that all knew it was an odious deal that would likely have been stopped through public pressure, both from Khadr's angry and shocked victims in the United States and from concerned Canadian citizens, including the Conservatives' own voting base. The secrecy of the deal is proof in itself of its flaws.

But that's Canada's political escape hatch. Canada's negotiators – soft-hearted or soft-headed diplomats – can legitimately claim that they simply didn't know any better. Perhaps they had read too many of the glowing letters of reference for Khadr. The ones masquerading as news reports.

But even the most naive Khadr sympathizers would have been shocked into sobriety had they learned the depth of Khadr's depravity as documented in Dr. Welner's report.

The only thing that's harder for a government than doing the right thing is doing the right thing *after* they have announced they're going to do the wrong thing. Because by then, it's not about the right public policy or what's best for Canada, it's about losing face and looking wobbly. For normal people, admitting a mistake is a sign of honesty and reasonableness. For a government, it's a nearly impossible admission of imperfection.

But, unpleasant as it may seem, that is exactly what Ottawa needs to do now in order to uphold Canadian security and protect the Canadian public. The cost of the Conservative government refusing to admit Khadr can be predicted: President Obama will be miffed and the army of Khadr apologists will scream bloody murder. The CBC will lead with the story for weeks, the *Toronto Star* will have a special edition dedicated to him, and Judy Rebick will go on a hunger strike.

No government – not even a Conservative one – really wants that kind of ugly spectacle.

But there are things that the Conservatives want even less. They don't want to destroy their hard-earned reputation for respecting and supporting the troops. How does welcoming home a soldier-murderer fit in with that reputation?

They don't want to be known as soft on crime. But how does voluntarily importing an unrepentant murderer – essentially springing him from jail – fit with that?

Unlike the professional protesters of the anti-war left, the silent majority of Canadians aren't used to going out and raising a mighty ruckus about their concerns: there are millions of people who have quietly, but resolutely, supported the War on Terror, the troops in Afghanistan, and tougher criminal justice laws. These are the very people who gave the Conservatives their majority government in 2011. For those severely normal Canadians to speak up – to flood their MPs' offices with phone calls and letters, to jam up talk radio call-in numbers, to write letters to the editor, to show up at MPs' town hall meetings, to even quit the Conservative Party and decline to make a political donation – that's the kind of action that people like Stephen Harper and Vic Toews and John Baird really pay attention to.

Doing a favour for President Obama is nice; but Obama doesn't vote in Canada, and he doesn't put up lawn signs or knock on doors or make political donations. Letting in Omar Khadr is a full-force slap in the face to the Conservative base in Canada. If enough ordinary Canadians express their outrage, the disapproval of Obama and the Canadian Bar Association will look like small potatoes.

More than 150 members of the Canadian Forces have died in Afghanistan, fighting shoulder to shoulder with U.S. servicemen like Sgt. Christopher Speer. Canada has proved time and again that we are loyal allies of the United States and the cause of freedom. Accepting the triumphant return of a murderous terrorist isn't a sign of our friendship with America – it's a sign of our moral weakness.

Canada deserves better.

ACKNOWLEDGEMENTS

Thank you to Jenny Bradshaw for her unlimited patience and to Kevin Libin for his indispensable help.

73 REASONS OMAR KHADR IS DANGEROUS, ACCORDING TO DR. MICHAEL WELNER

Undisputed Data Informing Opinion on Dangerousness
U.S. vs. Khadr
Michael Welner, M.D., October 26–27, 2010

1. To enhance the validity of any risk assessment, one combines clinical data that links to the specific context being examined with some kind of actuarial statistical measure together and embed it in the available literature and background that relates of the topic

2. The assessment of risk for a violent Jihadist has to be distinguished in context from that of risk of violence. Risk of radical jihadism is associated with actual violence as well as abetting violence, inspiring and fomenting violence, or financing or organizationally facilitating that violence

3. "Radical Islam" is differentiated from traditional Islam in that the ideology of radical Islam will not submit to living in a state or a world that is not governed by Sharia. The law of Islam is superior to the law of the state and radical Islam supports and employs even violent means in order to affect that turnover from civil law to a theocracy, whether it be in a particular country, whether it be in a particular region, or whether it be globally, depending on the individual and one's personal interests

4. Special considerations in the defendant's history are pertinent to risk assessment of a violent Jihadist

5. Omar Khadr has murdered

6. Omar Khadr has been part of al Qaeda, a terrorist organization

7. Khadr specifically engaged in hostilities on the day of the killing as an Islamist act of martyrdom

8. The United States continues to be at war with al Qaeda, and the war is not ending anytime soon

9. Omar Khadr was enmeshed and entangled with hardened JTF-Guantanamo Bay Camp 4 (Camp 4) Jihadists

10. Canadian officials visiting Khadr early in his Gitmo incarceration expressed concern for senior radicals acting as pseudoparents to him

11. Islamist radicalization is a serious problem in American prisons today

12. Khadr has significant stature among the al-Qaeda and Islamist detainees

13. Khadr drew great esteem from his father being a senior al-Qaeda leader

14. Khadr translated for his father when his father was operating for al-Qaeda in Afghanistan and Pakistan

15. Khadr has prior exposure and sophistication to the Jihadist movement

16. Khadr would not acknowledge his father's illegal choices and actions

17. Khadr's father had built a North American infrastructure for Islamist radicalism that is based in Toronto

18. Khadr has had exposure to fundraising for terrorist activity

19. Khadr has had exposure to money transfer for terrorist activity

20. Khadr bragged about killing an American soldier

21. Killing an American soldier is an extremely valued achievement in Camp 4

22. Khadr instigated antagonism among the detainees toward US personnel

23. Khadr was sought out by different blocs to be their block leader

24. Khadr was highly respected within the camp because of his devout observance

25. Khadr became more devout in custody

26. Khadr's interpretation of the Qu'ran was not out of line in any way with others in the Camp

27. Khadr was not open to any chaplain as a spiritual guide

28. Khadr was asked by other Jihadists to lead them in prayer, and did so

29. Khadr's greatest passions were devoted to study of the Qu'ran and devout Islam, rather than integrating into Canadian or alternative life orientation

30. While Khadr claimed he did not pursue Western studies because he needed a structured classroom setting, he was able to memorize the Qu'ran without such structure. This reflects he had far greater motivation and interest in pursuing religious values than Western values

31. Khadr, prior to negotiating a plea, showed no remorse for his bomb-making and bomb-laying activities

32. Khadr, prior to negotiating a plea, bragged about killing, showed no remorse for killing SFC Speer and denied killing SFC Speer even with defense mental health experts

33. Khadr did not want to confront his previous actions and blamed others for his actions on the videotape of his bomb-laying near Khowst

34. Khadr was resentful when put in a position to account for about his actions

35. Khadr blamed others for his confinement

36. Khadr resented being incarcerated for his actions

37. Khadr was resistant to discuss sensitive issues and mental health, even with defense witnesses who spent hundreds of hours with him

38. Issues Khadr did not process with psychologists or psychiatrists were his father's death and brothers' wounding at the hands of American-led forces

39. Psychological testing reflects Khadr as angry and manipulative

40. Khadr has an established international network of terrorist contacts

41. Khadr has a network of mainstream media propagandists who legitimize him

42. Khadr has the capacity to be inspiring to others in his potential for further jihad violence

43. Khadr's father and brother have a history of repatriation in Canada without being held accountable for terrorist activity. This weakens a deterrence against his return to activities of violent Jihad

44. Khadr's family remains highly radicalized

45. Khadr's brother has characterized theirs as an al-Qaeda family

46. Khadr's sister has spoken publicly of the exposure of the family's al-Qaeda legacy and having "to start from zero again"

47. Khadr has been closest to his highly radicalized family

48. Khadr remains protective of his highly radicalized family

49. Khadr remains responsible to his highly radicalized family

50. Khadr is expected to lead his family, and other siblings are less capable

51. Khadr's own defense team proposed deradicalization twice, most recently in 2009

52. The imam that the defense proposed for deradicalization in 2009 had a history of radical preaching and referring to President Obama as a "house slave"

53. There were no established programs of deradicalization in Canada in October 2010

54. Family and close acquaintances are instrumental in rooting an individual in Jihadism

55. Those with radicalized families are traditionally ineligible for established deradicalization programs

56. Deradicalization is typically only undertaken with inmates whose families reject their radicalism and are willing to take responsibility to ensure that the inmate does not return to radicalism

57. Education does not deradicalize so much as it represents a distraction

58. Deradicalization can only be undertaken with a prosocial Imam who interprets the Qu'ran peacefully

59. Deradicalization places the burden on the individual to demonstrate that he is deradicalized, not on society to pronounce someone deradicalized because of his own platitudes

60. Khadr's good prognostic factors are his physical resilience, socially agility, linguistic fluency, and street smarts

61. Identification with prosocial individuals is associated with a good prognosis

62. Anger and resentment is associated with a bad prognosis

63. Remorse is associated with a good prognosis

64. Identification with Western values is associated with a good prognosis

65. Officials of the Saudi deradicalization program have found that Guantanamo detainees return to terror activities more frequently than other detainees in their program

66. Guantanamo recidivism rates have substantially risen since these figures were first released

67. Return to hostilities is higher among those Guantanamo detainees who offended in their teens, as Khadr did

68. Belligerence toward the West among Guantanamo detainees is correlated with being from a Western country

69. U.S. Government statistics do not account for those who go from Guantanamo to other detention facilities abroad and so therefore have no opportunity to rejoin hostilities. This artificially lowers recidivism percentages

70. U.S. Government statistics do not account for those who change their names and locations and therefore would return to terrorism unaccounted. This artificially lowers recidivism percentages

71. U.S. Government statistics do not account for those who no longer engage in direct violence but are fomenting, facilitating and otherwise providing logistical support for terrorism. This artificially lowers recidivism percentages

72. Tracing released detainees does not involve the same mechanisms for tracking in developing countries. It is easy for released detainees to maintain an anonymous profile in Afghanistan, Pakistan, and other developing areas that would prevent their activities from being monitored. All of these individuals would be listed as non-recidivators. This artificially lowers recidivism percentages

73. U.S. Government statistics do not derive from many years after release, but rather months to a few years. With no long term data to account for those who eventually return to terrorism, Pentagon recidivism percentages are lower than they would be if measured over a longer term.

NOTES

CHAPTER 1

1. Shephard, Michelle. *Guantanamo's Child: The Untold Story of Omar Khadr* (John Wiley & Sons: Mississauga, Canada, 2008), p. vi.

2. Ibid., p. iv.

3. Ibid.

4. "Defiant Morgan: 'I will be vindicated over Iraq torture,'" PressGazette.com, September 3, 2004 (www.pressgazette.co.uk /story.asp?storyCode=26707&sectioncode=1).

5. Kurtz, Howard. "Newsweek apologizes," *The Washington Post*, May 16, 2005 (www.washingtonpost.com/wp-dyn/content /article/2005/05/15/AR2005051500605.html).

6. Ljunggren, David. "Canadian media glorify terror suspects – spy chief," Reuters, October 29, 2008 (http://uk.reuters.com /article/2009/10/29/idUKN29195720).

CHAPTER 2

1. Welner, Dr. Michael. Forensic Psychiatric Assessment of Omar Khadr, July 5, 2010.

2. Nickerson, Colin. "The Scarborough boy with blood on his hands," *Toronto Star*, March 9, 2003.

3. Shephard, Michelle. *Guantanamo's Child: The Untold Story of Omar Khadr* (John Wiley & Sons: Mississauga, Canada, 2008), p. 43.

4. CBC News Indepth: Khadr. "Al Qaeda family: The black sheep," March 3, 2004 (www.cbc.ca/news/background/khadr /alqaedafamily4.html).

5. Wright, Lawrence. *The Looming Tower* (Vintage Books: New York, 2006), p. 64.

6. Shephard. p. 29.

7. Shephard. p. 35.

8. Bell, Stewart. "Al-Qaeda's Canadian vanguard," *National Post*, September 6, 2002.

9. Emerson, Steven. *American Jihad* (Free Press: New York, 2006).

10. CBC News. "Khadr patriarch disliked Canada, says al-Qaeda biography," February 7, 2008 (www.cbc.ca/news/world /story/2008/02/07/khadr-bio.html).

11. Shephard, p. 45.

12. CNN. "Bomb rips Egyptian embassy," November 19, 1995 (www.cnn.com/WORLD/9511/pakistan_bomb/index.html).

13. Shephard, p. 47.

14. Bell, Stewart. "Al-Qaeda's Canadian vanguard," *National Post*, September 6, 2002.

15. Harito, Lori. "Khadr family history," Global News, October 9, 2009 (www.globalnews.ca/story.html?id=2068925).

16. www.cbc.ca/news/background/khadr/alqaedafamily2.html.

17. Shephard, p. 52.

18. Shephard, p. 52.

19. Bell, Stewart. "Al-Qaeda's Canadian vanguard," *National Post*, September 6, 2002.

20. Shephard, p. 54.

21. Bartleman, James. *Rollercoaster: My Hectic Years as Jean Chrétien's Diplomatic Advisor, 1994–1998* (Douglas Gibson Books: Toronto, 2005), p. 229.

22. Bell, Stewart. "Al-Qaeda's Canadian vanguard," *National Post*, September 6, 2002.

23. Pakistan Terrorist Groups. "Terrorist outfits: An overview," updated March 6, 2011 (www.satp.org/satporgtp/countries /pakistan/terroristoutfits/index.html).

24. Labott, Elise. "Report: Terror attacks up in Pakistan, Afghanistan," CNN News, April 30, 2009 (http://articles.cnn .com/2009-04-30/world/terrorism.report_1_afghan-border -terror-attacks-pakistani?_s=PM:WORLD).

25. Bell, Stewart. "Brother, sister probed for alleged terror ties," *National Post*, March 4, 2005.

26. Bell, Stewart. "'We're not al-Qaeda,' Khadr daughter says," *National Post*, May 19, 2004.

27. Bell, Stewart. "Sins of the father," *National Post*, October 16, 2010.

28. U.S. Treasury Department: Executive Order 13224 – Blocking Property and Prohibiting Transactions with Persons who Commit, Threaten to Commit, or Support Terrorism (2001) (www.scribd.com/doc/34559299/Executive-Order-13224).

29. Darling, Dan. "Al Qaeda's mad scientist," *Weekly Standard*, January 19, 2006.

30. Bell, Stewart. "Ahmed Khadr provided references for would-be terrorists," *National Post*, December 31, 2005.

31. Bell, Stewart. "Senior Khadr found Canada boring: book," *National Post*, February 6, 2008.

32. Bell, Stewart. "Charity funded jihad fighters," *National Post*, February 11, 2003.

33. Bell, Stewart. "Faction linked to Khadr claims attacks," *National Post*, July 13, 2006.

34. Ibid.

35. Ibid.

36. Bell, Stewart. "Khadr was dealing in missiles: affidavits," *National Post*, December 20, 2005.

37. Bell, Stewart. "Fake passport Khadr's plan to avoid U.S. justice," *National Post*, December 23, 2005.

38. Bell, Stewart. "Khadr was dealing in missiles: affidavits," *National Post*, December 20, 2005.

39. Ibid.

40. Ibid.

41. Bell, Stewart. "Brother, sister probed for alleged terror ties," *National Post*, March 4, 2005.

42. Bell, Stewart. "Canada liable for any abuse: Khadr lawyer warns," *National Post*, February 10, 2005.

43. Bell, Stewart. "Khadr son charged with sexual assault," *National Post*, June 15, 2010.

44. Shephard, p. 27.

45. Bell, Stewart. "Toronto teenager 'admits he's terrorist,'" *National Post,* September 17, 2004.

46. *USA v. Omar Khadr.* Stipulation of fact, October 13, 2010.

47. *USA v. Omar Khadr.* Stipulation of fact, October 13, 2010.

48. CBC News Indepth: Khadr. "Al-Qaeda family: The black sheep," March 4, 2004 (www.cbc.ca/news/background/khadr /alqaedafamily4.html).

CHAPTER 3

1. Confession of Omar Ahmed Khadr, October 13, 2010.

2. Mizrock, Azir. "Poll: 90% of ME views Jews unfavorably," *Jerusalem Post,* February 9, 2010 (www.jpost.com/Middle-East /Article.aspx?id=168176).

3. DellaPergola, Sergio. "World Jewish Population, 2010," Hebrew University of Jerusalem. Number 2. North American Jewish Data Bank. (www.jewishdatabank.org/Reports/World _Jewish_Population_2010.pdf).

4. Shephard, Michelle. *Guantanamo's Child: The Untold Story of Omar Khadr* (John Wiley & Sons; Mississauga, Canada, 2008), p. 26.

5. Ibid., p. 263.

6. "Canadian court denies Khadr extradition appeal," Agence France-Presse, May 7, 2011 (www.google.com/hostednews/afp /article/ALeqM5g2hooi31tDn6pWUKiNH5f5jm_6A?docId =CNG.oade78defc2875bf3eb3e6867300e47f.c41).

7. Anthony, Augustine. "Study ties new al Qaeda chief to murder of journalist Pearl," Reuters. May 23, 2011 (www.reuters.com/article/2011/05/23/us-pakistan-alqaeda -pearl-idUSTRE74M27020110523).

8. Ahlers, Mike, and Todd, Brian. "Al Qaeda group contemplated poisoning food in U.S., officials say," CNN, December 21, 2010 (http://articles.cnn.com/2010-12-21/us/al.qaeda.poison .plot_1_threat-stream-food-supply-al-qaeda-group?_s=PM:US).

9. Keteyian, Armen. "Latest terror threat in US aimed to poison food," CBS News, December 20, 2010 (www.cbsnews.com /stories/2010/12/20/eveningnews/main7169266.shtml).

10. Ahlers and Todd. "Al Qaeda group . . .".

11. Boettcher, Mike, and Schuster, Henry. "Al Qaeda terror strategy turns to assassination," CNN.com, January 22, 2003 (http://edition.cnn.com/2003/WORLD/asiapcf/central/01/22 /alqaeda.assassination.cnni/index.html).

12. "Timeline — Major attacks by al Qaeda," Reuters, May 2, 2011 (http://uk.reuters.com/article/2011/05/02/uk-binladen -qaeda-attacks-idUKTRE7413AE20110502).

13. "Al-Qaida claims Bhutto killing," Agence France-Presse, December 28, 2007 (www.ndtv.com/convergence/ndtv/story .aspx?id=NEWEN20070037061&ch=12/28/2007%208:21:00 %20AM).

14. Boettcher and Schuster. "Al Qaeda terror . . .".

15. Welner, Dr. Michael. Forensic Psychiatric Assessment of Omar Khadr, July 5, 2010.

16. Ibid.

17. Ibid.

18. Confession of Omar Ahmed Khadr, October 13, 2010.

19. Bell, Stewart. "Sex assault charges mark new chapter in Khadr family saga," *National Post*, June 15, 2010.

20. Bell, Stewart. "Mideast sources fund controversial mosque," *National Post*, January 20, 2011.

21. Welner. Forensic Psychiatric Assessment of Omar Khadr.

22. Confession of Omar Ahmed Khadr, October 13, 2010.

23. Welner. Forensic Psychiatric Assessment of Omar Khadr.

24. Ibid.

25. Department of Justice. "Producible documents" in connection with Omar Khadr welfare visit on March 12 and 14, 2008.

26. Report of welfare visit with Omar Khadr, April 8, 9, and 11, 2008.

27. *The Bridge* by Manfred Gregor (book review). *Time,* August 15, 1960 (www.time.com/time/magazine/article /0,9171,939797,00.html).

28. Welner. Forensic Psychiatric Assessment of Omar Khadr.

29. Confession of Omar Ahmed Khadr, October 13, 2010.

30. Welner. Forensic Psychiatric Assessment of Omar Khadr.

31. Ibid.

32. Ibid.

33. Confession of Omar Ahmed Khadr, October 13, 2010.

34. Ibid.

35. Ibid.

CHAPTER 4

1. CBC News Online feature: "Workplace safety" (www.cbc.ca /news/interactives/map-workplacesafety/).

2. CBC News Online feature: "In the line of duty: Canada's casualties" (www.cbc.ca/news/background/afghanistan /casualties/list.html).

3. Bencharif, Sarah- Taïssir. "Distant exposure to IEDs can leave soldiers with concussion; New Toronto study," *National Post*, May 6, 2011.

4. Bowden, Mark. "The Desert One debacle," *The Atlantic*, May 2006.

5. Haney, Eric. *Inside Delta Force: The Story of America's Elite Counterterrorist Unit* (Dell: New York, 2003), p. 400.

6. Shephard, Michelle. *Guantanamo's Child: The Untold Story of Omar Khadr* (John Wiley & Sons: Mississauga, Canada, 2008), p. 7.

7. Mayeda, Andrew. Eulogy for Christopher Speer, tabled at Omar Khadr sentencing hearing, *Vancouver Sun* blog. October 27, 2010 (http://communities.canada.com /vancouversun/print.aspx?postid=707400).

8. Affidavit of Tabitha Speer: *Layne Morris, Tabitha Speer, Estate of Christopher Speer, Taryn Speer and Tanner Peer vs. Ahmad Said Khadr*, November 11, 2005.

9. Ibid.

10. Shephard, p. 2.

11. http://topics.nytimes.com/top/news/newyorkandregion /series/portraits_of_grief/index.html.

12. Letters from Speer's children, *Toronto Star* online (www.thestar.com/staticcontent/883614).

CHAPTER 5

1. Parliamentary testimony, May 13, 2008.

2. Ibid., May 27, 2008.

CHAPTER 6

1. Kent, Tom. "Canada is much more than a hotel," *The Globe and Mail*, April 26, 2008, p. A25.

2. Gunter, Lorne. "Whiners: Find your own way out of Beirut," *Edmonton Journal*, July 21, 2006.

3. Shephard, Michelle. *Guantanamo's Child: The Untold Story of Omar Khadr* (John Wiley & Sons: Mississauga, Canada, 2008), p. 27.

4. Ibid., pp. 35–36.

5. Simons, Paula. "Omar Khadr's tragic story mostly about child abuse," *Edmonton Journal*, June 30, 2007.

6. Mahmoud, Tahir. "Canadian government deprives own citizen, Omar Khadr, of basic rights," *Crescent International* (www.crescenticit.com/component/content/article/2672 -=canadian-government-deprives-own-citizen-omar-khadr -of-basic-rights.html).

7. "No more clemency appeals for Canadians on death row in U.S.: Tories," CBC News, November 1, 2007 (www.cbc.ca/news /canada/story/2007/11/01/death-penalty.html).

8. Libin, Kevin. "Home, not free," *National Post*, June 5, 2010, p. A8.

9. Kidd, Kenneth. "From 'citizen' to 'passport': A complicated existence," *Toronto Star*, July 30, 2006, p. D1.

10. http://www.cic.gc.ca/english/pdf/pub/discover.pdf.

11. Kent. "Canada is much more . . .".

12. Cohen, Andrew. "A guide to what is expected in Canada," *Windsor Star*, November 30, 2009, p. A8.

13. Fitzpatrick, Meagan. "Trudeau retracts 'barbaric' remarks," CBC News, March 15, 2011 (www.cbc.ca/news/politics /story/2011/03/15/pol-trudeau-barbaric.html).

CHAPTER 7

1. Friscolanti, Michael. "The House of Khadr," *Maclean's*, August 4, 2006.

2. Rosenberg, Carol. "No ice cream on stick for Guantánamo detainees," *Miami Herald*, October 12, 2010.

3. Howard, Manny. "The Guantanamo thirteen," *Slate*, May 29, 2003 (www.slate.com/id/2083612/).

4. "The last frontier," *Economist*, December 30, 2009 (www.economist.com/node/15173037).

5. UNICEF: Country Statistics, Afghanistan (www.unicef.org /infobycountry/afghanistan_statistics.html).

6. Doran, Jamie. "Behind Taliban lines," PBS *Frontline*, aired February 23, 2010.

7. Glazov, Jamie. "Boys of the Taliban," FrontPageMag.com, January 1, 2007 (http://archive.frontpagemag.com/readArticle .aspx?ARTID=852).

8. Bell, Katie, et al. "Former army prosecutor: Some prisoners 'asked to stay in Gitmo' rather than go home," CNSNews.com, June 30, 2011 (www.cnsnews.com/news/article/former-army -prosecutor-some-prisoners-as).

9. Perkel, Colin. "Mom of teen charged at Guantanamo says Ottawa in cahoots with American 'gods,'" Canadian Press Newswire, November 9, 2005.

10. *USA v. Omar Khadr*. Stipulation of fact, October 13, 2010.

11. "Captives told to claim torture," *Washington Times*, May 31, 2005 (www.washingtontimes.com/news/2005/may/31 /20050531-121655-7932r/).

12. Ibid.

13. Sutton, Jane. "Weigh-in tape shows Omar Khadr's life at Guantanamo," Reuters, August 9, 2010 (www.reuters.com /article/2010/08/09/us-guantanamo-canadian-idUS TRE6784JW20100809).

14. Welner, Dr. Michael. Forensic Psychiatric Assessment of Omar Khadr, July 5, 2010, p. 60.

15. Howard. "The Guantanamo thirteen."

16. Cucullu, Gordon. *Inside Gitmo* (HarperCollins: New York, 2009), p. 151.

17. Ibid., p. 151.

18. Ibid., p. 152.

19. Howard. "The Guantanamo thirteen."

20. Cucullu. *Inside Gitmo*, p. 152.

21. Ibid., p. 154.

22. Bowker, David, and Kay, David. "Guantánamo by the numbers," *The New York Times*, November 10, 2007.

23. "Facts," *New Internationalist Magazine*, Issue 300, April 1998 (www.newint.org/features/1998/04/05/facts/).

24. Welner. Forensic Psychiatric Assessment of Omar Khadr, p. 12.

25. Norton-Taylor, Richard. "Guantánamo is gulag of our time, says Amnesty," *The Guardian,* May 26, 2005 (www.guardian .co.uk/world/2005/may/26/usa.guantanamo).

26. Rosenberg, Carol. "Convicts break monotony with Bush memoir, Shakespeare," *Miami Herald,* February 28, 2011.

27. Cucullu. *Inside Gitmo,* p. 142.

28. Bowker and Kay. "Guantánamo by the numbers."

29. Cucullu. *Inside Gitmo,* p. xxii.

30. Ibid., p. 150–152.

31. Government of Canada. Report of Welfare Visit with Omar Khadr, Consular Affairs Case Management, November 7 and 9, 2007.

32. Donnelly, Tom, and McCaffrey, Ret. Gen. Barry. "McCaffrey visits Guantanamo," *Armed Forces Journal,* July 2006.

33. Herridge, Catherine. Fox News Radio report, July 15, 2010 (www.redlasso.com/ClipPlayer.aspx?id=bfc28cf3-85ac-48 -ec-9aa3-35d5a3275335).

34. Department of Justice. "Producible documents" in connection with Omar Khadr welfare visit on March 12 and 14, 2008.

35. Government of Canada. Report of Welfare Visit with Omar Khadr.

36. Department of Justice. "Producible documents" from welfare visit on March 12 and 14, 2008.

37. Friscolanti, Michael. "What did Ottawa buy Omar Khadr?" *Maclean's*, May 25, 2010.

38. Ibid.

39. Ibid.

40. Department of Justice. Report of Welfare Visit with Omar Khadr, May 7, 8, and 9, 2008.

41. Cucullu. *Inside Gitmo*, p. 156.

42. Ibid., p. 156.

43. Ibid., p. 158.

44. Ibid., p. 156.

45. Report of Welfare Visit with Omar Khadr, April 8, 9, and 11, 2009.

46. Welner. Forensic Psychiatric Assessment of Omar Khadr, p. 62.

47. Ibid.

48. Cullucu. *Inside Gitmo*, p. 162.

49. Government of Canada. Report of Welfare Visit with Omar Khadr, November 7 and 9, 2007.

50. Welfare Visit reports.

51. Welfare Visit reports.

52. Perkel. "Mom of teen charged . . .".

53. Welner. Forensic Psychiatric Assessment of Omar Khadr, p. 15.

54. Ibid., p. 15.

55. Ruling: *USA v. Omar Khadr*, Suppression motions D-094, D-111.

56. Ibid.

57. Coursen-Neff, Zama. "The Taliban's war on education: Schoolgirls are still under fire in Afghanistan," *Los Angeles Times*, July 31, 2006.

CHAPTER 8

1. Weir, Ivy. "A young Canadian abandoned by his country," *The Record* (Sherbrooke), December 31, 2010

2. Martin, Lawrence. "In the matter of Omar Khadr, shame on us," *The Globe and Mail*, July 15, 2010.

3. Walkom, Thomas. "Khadr heading for a U.S. kangaroo court," *Toronto Star*, November 14, 2009.

4. Martin. "In the matter of Omar Khadr . . .".

5. Confession of Omar Ahmed Khadr, October 13, 2010.

6. Walkom. "Khadr heading for . . .".

7. Walkom, Thomas. "Khadr shows peril of rush to judgment," *Toronto Star*, February 9, 2008.

8. Weir. "A young Canadian . . .".

9. Lakritz, Naomi. "Khadr denied justice," *Calgary Herald*, July 24, 2008.

10. BBC News. "Profile: Key US terror suspects," February 11, 2008 (http://news.bbc.co.uk/2/hi/5322694.stm).

11. Jeffrey, Terence P. "CIA confirms: Waterboarding 9/11 mastermind led to info that aborted 9/11-style attack on Los Angeles," CNSNews.com, April 21, 2009 (www.cnsnews.com /node/46949).

12. Wead, Cdr. Frank "Spig." "Waterboarding: A SERE-ing experience for tens of thousands of US military personnel," *Human Events*, November 5, 2007 (www.humanevents.com /article.php?id=23220).

13. "Captives told to claim torture," *Washington Times*, May 31, 2005 (www.washingtontimes.com/news/2005/may/31/20050531 -121655-7932r/).

14. Ibid.

15. "From insects to waterboarding: 10 'torture' techniques blessed by Bush," Sunday *Times*, April 17, 2009 (www.times -online.co.uk/tol/news/world/us_and_americas/article6111109.ece).

16. "Egypt's torture victims describe beatings, electroshock, rape threats," ABC News, February 3, 2011 (http://abcnews.go.com /Blotter/egypts-torture-victims-describe-beatings-electroshock -rape-threats/story?id=12821831).

17. "Torture and impunity in Jordan's prisons," Human Rights Watch, October 8, 2008 (www.hrw.org/en/node/75506/section/7).

18. Greenwald, Glenn. "U.S. teenager tortured in Kuwait and barred re-entry into the U.S.," Salon.com, January 6, 2011 (www.salon.com/news/opinion/glenn_greenwald/2011/01 / 06/kuwait).

19. Welner, Dr. Michael. Forensic Psychiatric Assessment of Omar Khadr, July 5, 2010, p. 7.

20. Ibid.

21. Ibid., p. 61.

22. Ibid., pp. 10, 14.

23. Ibid., p. 58.

24. "Students rally in support of Omar Khadr in Edmonton," *Edmonton Journal*, November 9, 2008 (www.canada.com /montrealgazette/story.html?id=15203a37-9ec7-4333-a348-b67 ece676a86).

25. "The Atkinson principles," *Toronto Star*, November 24, 2008 (www.thestar.com/article/542441–the-atkinson-principles).

26. Tweet by Michelle Shephard, October 27, 2010 (http://twitter.com/#!/shephardm/status/28903178965).

27. FP Infomart search.

28. Shephard, Michelle. *Guantanamo's Child: The Untold Story of Omar Khadr* (John Wiley & Sons: Mississauga, Canada, 2008).

29. Levant, Ezra. "Coddled Khadr," *Toronto Sun*, October 26, 2010.

30. Rebick, Judy. "My heart aches for Omar Khadr," Rabble.ca, July 8, 2010 (http://rabble.ca/blogs/bloggers/judes/2010/07 /my-heart-aches-omar-khadar).

31. Shephard. *Guantanamo's Child*, p. 2.

CHAPTER 9

1. "Q&A: 'We must wake up': Michael Ignatieff reflects on Canada's place in the post-Sept. 11 world," *Maclean's*, February 4, 2002.

2. Valpy, Michael. "You've come a long way Iggy. But is it far enough?" *The Globe and Mail*, August 28, 2010, p. F1.

3. El Akkad, Omar. "Khadr likely to leave Gitmo soon after Obama inauguration," *The Globe and Mail*, January 15, 2009, p. A5.

4. El Akkad, Omar and Daniel Leblanc. "Ottawa 'reassessing' Khadr's case, MacKay says," *The Globe and Mail*, January 22, 2009, p. A1.

5. "Canadian teen held by U.S. military," CBC News online, September 6, 2002 (www.cbc.ca/news/world/story/2002/09/05 /canadian_teen020905.htm).

6. Freeze, Colin. "Bring back Khadr now, Martin says," *The Globe and Mail*, July 21, 2008, p. A4.

7. Letter from the Leader of the Opposition, Stéphane Dion, to the Prime Minister, Stephen Harper, July 29, 2008.

8. Cotler, Irwin. "The least we can do in the case of Omar Khadr," *The Vancouver Sun*, January 27, 2009.

9. Ibid.

10. "Obama ratifies Bush," *Wall Street Journal*, March 8, 2011.

11. Letter from the Leader of the Opposition, Stéphane Dion, to the Prime Minister, Stephen Harper, July 29, 2008.

12. http://www.youtube.com/watch?v=yNCyrFV2G_o.

13. Gordon, Sean. "Khadr's supporters lash out at Ottawa," *Toronto Star*, November 9, 2005.

14. *The Globe and Mail*, February 10, 2005.

15. "Ottawa accused of not helping Canadian held at Guantanamo charged with murder," CBC News online, November 9, 2005.

16. Gordon. "Khadr's supporters . . .".

17. "Pettigrew not surprised Canadian won't face death penalty in U.S.," *North Bay Nugget*, November 11, 2005.

18. "Mom of teen charged at Guantanamo says Ottawa in cahoots with American 'gods,'" Canadian Press Newswire, November 9, 2005.

19. "MP wants Khadrs charged under anti-terror laws," Canadian Press, April 16, 2004.

20. "Omar Khadr: The youngest terrorist?" CBS: 60 *Minutes*, November 18, 2007.

21. "Canadian teen held by U.S. will get consular help," *Daily News* (Truro), September 7, 2002.

22. Freeze. "Bring back Khadr . . .".

23. Makin, Kirk. "Canadian Bar Association moves to support rights of Khadr," *The Globe and Mail*, August. 11, 2007 (www.theglobeandmail.com/news/national/article775596.ece).

24. "CBA calls for Omar Khadr to be released from Guantanamo Bay and turned over to Canada," CBA Press Release, August 12, 2007; January 23, 2009, letter to Prime Minister Stephen Harper from CBA president J. Guy Joubert and others (www.cba.org/CBA/News/2007_releases/2007-08-12 _omar.aspx) (www.cba.org/CBA/submissions/pdf/09-02-eng.pdf).

25. "Human Rights in Myanmar: Overview," Amnesty International (www.amnesty.ca/themes/myanmar_overview.php).

26. O'Brien, Harriet. "Suu Kyi urges Britons to boycott Burma," *The Independent*, March 17, 1996 (www.independent.co.uk/news /world/suu-kyi-urges-britons-to-boycott-burma-1342477.html).

27. "China Human Rights," Amnesty International (www.amnesty usa.org/our-work/countries/asia-and-the-pacific/china).

CHAPTER 10

1. Welner, Dr. Michael. Forensic Psychiatric Assessment of Omar Khadr, July 5, 2010.

2. http://www.trialadvice.com.

3. Perkel, Colin. "Theatre-arts grad helps defence pick Omar Khadr jury from 11 men, four women," Canadian Press (via CTV website), August 10, 2010 (www.ctvbc.ctv.ca/servlet /an/local/CTVNews/20100810/100810_khadr/20100810/ ?hub =CP24Home).

4. Becker, Jo. "What can Khadr's jury tell us about Guantanamo justice?" Human Rights Watch, *Huffington Post,* August 13, 2010 (www.huffingtonpost.com /jo-becker/what-can-khadrs-jury-tell_b_681724.html).

5. Interview with trial witness, July 5, 2011.

6. Gordon, Jerry. "Omar Khadr's Hail Mary (Allah) pass at GITMO tribunal," *New English Review,* April 2011 (www.newenglishreview.org/custpage.cfm/frm/87683 /sec_id/87683).

7. Walkom, Thomas. "Omar Khadr's Guantanamo show trial," *Toronto Star,* October 10, 2010 (www.thestar.com/news/canada /article/883469–walkom-omar-khadr-s-guantanamo-show-trial).

8. Isikoff, Michael. "Hillary Clinton helped engineer 'boy soldier' plea deal," NBC News, October 25, 2010 (www.msnbc .msn.com/id/39834263/ns/us_news-security/t/hillary-clinton -helped-engineer-boy-soldier-plea-deal/).

9. Cooper, Elise. "Victim of teen terrorist Khadr rips plea deal," FrumForum.com, November 6, 2010 (www.frumforum.com /victim-of-teen-terrorist-khadr-rips-plea-deal).

10. Ibid.

11. Gordon. "Omar Khadr's Hail Mary (Allah) pass . . .".

12. Testimony of Dr. Michael Welner; sentencing hearing for Omar Khadr. Guantanamo Bay, Cuba, October 26, 2010.

13. Ibid.

14. Ibid.

15. Ibid., p. 50, 51.

16. Ibid.

17. Response from Dr. Welner to Defense Motion for Clemency.

18. Testimony of Dr. Michael Welner; sentencing hearing for Omar Khadr. Guantanamo Bay, Cuba, October 26, 2010.

19. Ibid.

20. Ibid.

21. Ibid.

22. Ibid., p. 58.

23. CBC News Indepth: "The William Sampson story," June 14, 2006 (www.cbc.ca/news/background/sampson/).

24. Meissner, Christian A., and Albrechtsen, Justin S. "Interrogation and torture," on *AccessScience* website (McGraw-Hill Companies, 2007) (http://www.accessscience.com).

25. Testimony of Dr. Michael Welner, p. 58.

26. Ibid., p. 16.

27. Ibid., p. 61.

28. Ibid.

29. Ibid., pp. 10, 14, 22.

30. Ibid., p. 49.

31. Ibid., p. 52.

32. Ibid., p. 39.

33. Ibid.

34. Ibid., p. 15.

35. Ibid., p. 46.

36. Ibid.

37. Ibid.

38. Ibid., p. 10.

39. Ibid., p. 60.

40. Ibid., p. 21.

41. Ibid., p. 47.

42. Shephard, Michelle. *Guantanamo's Child: The Untold Story of Omar Khadr* (John Wiley & Sons: Mississauga, Canada, 2008), p. iv.

43. Ibid., p. v.

44. Testimony of Dr. Michael Welner, p. 47.

45. Ibid., p. 48.

46. Letter from Dr. Michael Welner to Vice Admiral Bruce MacDonald. Re: *USA v. Omar Khadr*, April 14, 2011, p. 10.

47. Ibid.

CHAPTER 11

1. Tapper, Jake. "Hoekstra on Underwear Bomber: 'We missed him at every step,'" ABC News, "Political Punch" blog, December 28, 2009 (http://blogs.abcnews.com/political punch/2009/12/hoekstra-on-underwear-bomber-we-missed-him-at-every-step.html).

2. Ross, Brian. "Al Qaeda leader behind Northwest Flight 253 terror plot was released by U.S.," ABC News. December 28, 2009 (http://abcnews.go.com/Blotter/men-believed-northwest-airlines-plot-set-free/story?id=9434065).

3. Ibid.

4. Bennet, Brian. "Many freed Guantanamo inmates join terrorists, files say," *Los Angeles Times*, April 25, 2011 (http://articles.latimes.com/2011/apr/25/world/la-fg-yemen -wikileaks-20110426).

5. Goldman, Russell. "Does rehab for terrorists work?" ABC News, January 1, 2010 (http://abcnews.go.com/International /guantanamo-release-saudi-rehab-ali-al-shihri-now/ story?id=9458164).

6. Coghlan, Tom. "Freed Guantánamo inmates are heading for Yemen to join al-Qaeda fight," *The Sunday Times*, January 5, 2010 (www.timesonline.co.uk/tol/news/world/middle_east /article6975971.ece).

7. Lappin, Yaakov. "Analysis: Al-Qaida exploiting failed states for sovereignty," *Jerusalem Post*, May 30, 2011 (www.jpost.com /MiddleEast/Article.aspx?id=222778&R=R3).

8. Worth, Robert F. "Freed by the U.S., Saudi becomes a Qaeda chief," *The New York Times*, January 22, 2009.

9. Center for Constitutional Rights. Press Release: "CCR denounces blanket decision not to release Guantánamo detainees to Yemen," January 5, 2010 (http://ccrjustice.org /newsroom/press-releases/ccr-denounces-blanket-decision -not-release-guant%C3%A1namo-detainees-yemen).

10. Welner, Dr. Michael. Forensic Psychiatric Assessment of Omar Khadr, July 5, 2010.

11. Director of National Intelligence. Summary of the Reengagement of Detainees Formerly Held at Guantanamo Bay, Cuba, 2010.

12. Bergen, Peter, et al. "How many Gitmo alumni take up arms," New America Foundation, January 11, 2011.

13. All recidivism reports. New America Foundation. January 11, 2011.

14. Director of National Intelligence. Summary of the Reengagement of Detainees Formerly Held at Guantanamo Bay, Cuba, 2010.

15. Hesterman, Jennifer L. "Catch and release Jihadist recidivism," Homeland1.com, May 4, 2010 (www.homeland1.com/domestic-international-terrorism/articles/815413-Catch-and-release-Jihadist-recidivism/).

16. Poniewozik, James. "Calling the c-word the c-word," *Time*, June 18, 2002 (www.time.com/time/columnist/poniewozik/article/0,9565,263504,00.html).

17. Hesterman. "Catch and release . . .".

18. "Omar Khadr: The youngest terrorist?" CBS News: 60 Minutes, February 11, 2009 (www.cbsnews.com/ stories/2007/11/16/60minutes/main3516048_page3.shtml ?tag=contentMain;contentBody).

19. "Interview: Maha Elsamnah and Zaynab Khadr," PBS Frontline (www.pbs.org/wgbh/pages/frontline/shows/khadr /interviews/mahazaynab.html).

20. Tyler, Tracey. "Don't let Khadr brother walk free, court urged," Toronto Star, April 7, 2011.

21. Blazing Catfur. Screen capture of Zaynab Khadr's Facebook page, May 14, 2011.

22. Dennis Edney and Zafar Bangash press conference. February 11, 2009.

CHAPTER 12

1. www.maherarar.net.

2. Steel, Kevin. "What really happened to Maher Arar?" Western Standard, February 26, 2007.

3. El Akkad, Omar, and Freeze, Colin. "Testimony puts Arar, Khadr at al-Qaeda safehouse," The Globe and Mail, January 20, 2009.

4. Dube, Francine. "Arars sue Canada for $400M in damages: Allege negligence in targeting Ottawan for investigation," *National Post.* April 22, 2004.

5. "$10.5 million in compensation will help rebuild his life, says Arar," Canwest News Service, January 26, 2007 (www.canada .com/topics/news/story.html?id=afdc7d48-2ofe-4111-b325 -c55c79099d8f&k=98472).

6. Freeze, Colin. "Omar Khadr's civil suit against Ottawa seeks $10-million," *The Globe and Mail,* February 5, 2010.

7. "Arar's wife Monia Mazigh to seek NDP nomination," CTV News, March 10, 2004 (www.ctv.ca/servlet/ArticleNews /mini/CTVNews/20040310/monia_ndp_arar_040310?s _name= . . . &no_ads=).

8. Gordon, Mary. "Now she's fighting to be an MP: Monia Mazigh fought hard to free husband Maher Arar from a Syrian jail," *Toronto Star*, June 28, 2004, p. A9.

9. Macleod, Ian. "Arar launches e-magazine to monitor security practices" *Montreal Gazette*, January 21, 2010, p. A13.

10. Botting, Garry. "Canada's extradition law: The least fair act on Earth?" *Prism*, June 17, 2011 (http://prism-magazine. com/2011/06/canadas-extradition-law-the-least-fair-act-on-earth/).

11. Neve, Alex. "From 2002 to 2010: Canada must end complicity in torture," *Prism*, February 17, 2010 (http://prism-magazine.com/2010/02/from-2002-to-2010-canada-must-end-complicity-in-torture/).

12. www.maherarar.net/interview%20request.php.

13. Mazigh, Monia. *Hope & Despair* (McClelland & Stewart: Toronto, 2007), p. xii.

14. Pratt, Sheila. "Edmonton professor, Khadr exchanged letters for two years," *Edmonton Journal*, December 28, 2010 (www.edmontonjournal.com/news/Edmonton+professor+Khadr+exchanged+letters+years/3749790/story.html).

15. Weese, Bryn. "Khadr to attend school in Edmonton?" *Toronto Sun*, October 28, 2010 (www.torontosun.com/news/canada/2010/10/28/15861156.html).

16. King's University College News Release: "King's hosts Dennis Edney, lawyer for Omar Khadr during its Interdisciplinary Studies Conference," September 9, 2008 (www.kingsu.ca/news/pdf/IS-Conference-Kings_Sept9-08.pdf).

17. McLeod, Shane. "Speak out Edmonton for human rights and the repatriation of Omar Khadr," Facebook Group Announcement (www.facebook.com/topic.php?uid=49663170743&topic=6172).

18. Pratt. "Edmonton professor, Khadr . . .".

19. Weese. "Khadr to attend school . . .".

20. U.S. Department of Defense. Office of the Assistant
Secretary of Defense (Public Affairs). News Release No.
1003-10: "Details of Omar Khadr Plea Agreement Released,"
October 31, 2010 (www.defense.gov/releases/release.aspx
?releaseid=14024).

21. Canadian Islamic Congress. News Release: "Islamic
Congress Condemns Federal Government's Inaction on Omar
Khadr Case," July 16, 2008 (www.canadianislamiccongress.com
/cic2010/2008/07/16/islamic-congress-condemns-federal
-governments-inaction-on-omar-khadr-case/).

22. Canadian Arab Federation. News Release: "CAF calls upon
Prime Minister to uphold Omar Khadr's basic Charter rights,"
April 24, 2009 (www.caf.ca/Admin.aspx?AppModule=TxApp
Framework.Web.Admin&Command=EMBEDDEDFILE&
DataObjectID=701&ColumnID=3581&FieldName
=CONTENT&Lang=EN&RecordID=2009).

23. Ryerson University website (www.ryerson.ca/socialjustice
/about/judy_rebick/index.html).

24. "Court lifts all restrictions on Karla Homolka," CTV News,
December 1, 2005 (www.ctv.ca/CTVNews/Toronto
Home/20051130/homolka_judge_051130/).

25. Porges, Marisa L. "The Saudi deradicalization experiment,"
Council on Foreign Relations, January 22, 2010.

26. Taylor, Frederick. *Exorcising Hitler: The Occupation and Denazification of Germany* (Bloomsbury Press: New York, 2011).

27. Dennis Edney and Zafar Bangash press conference, February 11, 2009.

28. Coren, Michael. "Problem? Judge for yourself," *Toronto Sun*, February 10, 2007.

29. Bell, Stewart. "Call to jihad from a Markham strip mall," *National Post*, April 6, 2002, p. B1.

30. Ibid.

31. Brean, Joseph. "Conspiracies, propaganda top agenda at Islam summit," *National Post*, February 16, 2010, p. A1.

32. Bell. "Call to jihad . . .".

33. Testimony of Dr. Michael Welner; Sentence Hearing: *USA v. Omar Khadr*, October 26, 2010.

34. Mayeda, Andrew. "Khadr tells soldier's widow he's 'really sorry for the pain I've caused'," Postmedia News, October 28, 2010 (www.ottawacitizen.com/story_print.html?id=3740827 &sponsor=).

35. Ibid.

36. Testimony of Dr. Michael Welner; Sentence Hearing: *USA v. Omar Khadr*, October 26, 2010.

37. Ibid.

38. Ibid.

39. Ibid.

40. Ibid.

41. Ibid.

42. Ibid.

43. Ibid.

44. Letter from Dr. Michael Welner to Vice Admiral Bruce MacDonald. Re: *USA v. Omar Khadr*, April 14, 2011, p. 9.

45. Ibid.

46. Welner, Dr. Michael. Forensic Psychiatric Assessment of Omar Khadr, July 5, 2010.

47. Testimony of Dr. Michael Welner; Sentence Hearing: *USA v. Omar Khadr*, October 26, 2010.

CHAPTER 13

1. Teotonio, Isabel. "Life term for terror ringleader," *Toronto Star*, January 19, 2010 (www.thestar.com/news/gta/crime /article/752507–life-term-for-terror-ringleader).

2. *USA v. Omar Ahmed Khadr*. Offer for pre-trial agreement, October 13, 2010.

3. Graham, Laurie. "Khadr coming home after pleading guilty at Guantanamo Bay," CBC's *The National*, October 25, 2010.

4. "Serial killer Clifford Olson denied parole," CBC News, November 30, 2010 (www.cbc.ca/news/canada/montreal /story/2010/11/30/serial-killer-clifford-olson-parole-hearing.html).